PERSPECTIVES 1

Lewis **LANSFORD**

Daniel **BARBER**

Amanda **JEFFRIES**

NATIONAL
GEOGRAPHIC
LE**A**RNING

Australia • Brazil • Mexico • Singapore • United Kingdom • United States

Perspectives 1b Combo Split
Lewis Lansford, Daniel Barber, Amanda Jeffries

Publisher: Sherrise Roehr

Executive Editor: Sarah Kenney

Publishing Consultant: Karen Spiller

Senior Development Editor: Brenden Layte

Development Editor: Lewis Thompson

Editorial Assistant: Gabe Feldstein

Director of Global Marketing: Ian Martin

Product Marketing Manager: Anders Bylund

Director of Content and Media Production:
Michael Burggren

Production Manager: Daisy Sosa

Media Researcher: Leila Hishmeh

Manufacturing Customer Account Manager:
Mary Beth Hennebury

Art Director: Brenda Carmichael

Production Management and Composition:
Lumina Datamatics, Inc.

Cover Image: Bernardo Galmarini/
Alamy Stock Photo

For product information and technology assistance, contact us at
Cengage Learning Customer & Sales Support, cengage.com/contact

For permission to use material from this text or product,
submit all requests online at **cengage.com/permissions**
Further permissions questions can be emailed to
permissionrequest@cengage.com

Student Edition: Level 1 Combo Split B
ISBN: 978-1-337-29739-4

National Geographic Learning
20 Channel Center Street
Boston, MA 02210
USA

National Geographic Learning, a Cengage Learning Company, has a mission to bring the world to the classroom and the classroom to life. With our English language programs, students learn about their world by experiencing it. Through our partnerships with National Geographic and TED Talks, they develop the language and skills they need to be successful global citizens and leaders.

Locate your local office at **international.cengage.com/region**

Visit National Geographic Learning online at **NGL.Cengage.com/ELT**
Visit our corporate website at **www.cengage.com**

Printed in China
Print Number: 01 Print Year: 2018

ACKNOWLEDGMENTS

Paulo Rogerio Rodrigues
Escola Móbile, São Paulo, Brazil

Claudia Colla de Amorim
Escola Móbile, São Paulo, Brazil

Antonio Oliveira
Escola Móbile, São Paulo, Brazil

Rory Ruddock
Atlantic International Language Center, Hanoi, Vietnam

Carmen Virginia Pérez Cervantes
La Salle, Mexico City, Mexico

Rossana Patricia Zuleta
CIPRODE, Guatemala City, Guatemala

Gloria Stella Quintero Riveros
Universidad Católica de Colombia, Bogotá, Colombia

Mónica Rodriguez Salvo
MAR English Services, Buenos Aires, Argentina

Itana de Almeida Lins
Grupo Educacional Anchieta, Salvador, Brazil

Alma Loya Alma Loya
Colegio de Chihuahua, Chihuahua, Mexico

María Trapero Dávila
Colegio Teresiano, Ciudad Obregon, Mexico

Silvia Kosaruk
Modern School, Lanús, Argentina

Florencia Adami
Dámaso Centeno, Caba, Argentina

Natan Galed Gomez Cartagena
Global English Teaching, Rionegro, Colombia

James Ubriaco
Colégio Santo Agostinho, Belo Horizonte, Brazil

Ryan Manley
The Chinese University of Hong Kong, Shenzhen, China

Silvia Teles
Colégio Cândido Portinari, Salvador, Brazil

María Camila Azuero Gutiérrez
Fundación Centro Electrónico de Idiomas, Bogotá, Colombia

Martha Ramirez
Colegio San Mateo Apostol, Bogotá, Colombia

Beata Polit
XXIII LO Warszawa, Poland

Beata Tomaszewska
V LO Toruń, Poland

Michał Szkudlarek
I LO Brzeg, Poland

Anna Buchowska
I LO Białystok, Poland

Natalia Maćkowiak
one2one, Kosakowo, Poland

Agnieszka Dończyk
one2one, Kosakowo, Poland

Perspectives teaches learners to think critically and to develop the language skills they need to find their own voice in English. The carefully-guided language lessons, real-world stories, and TED Talks motivate learners to think creatively and communicate effectively.

In *Perspectives*, learners develop:

● AN OPEN MIND

Every unit explores one idea from different perspectives, giving learners opportunities for practicing language as they look at the world in new ways.

● A CRITICAL EYE

Students learn the critical thinking skills and strategies they need to evaluate new information and develop their own opinions and ideas to share.

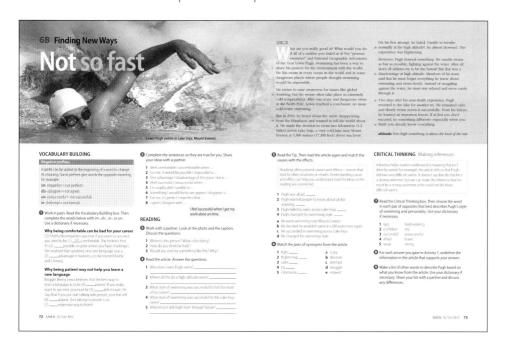

● A CLEAR VOICE

Students respond to the unit theme and express their own ideas confidently in English.

CONTENTS

6 Do Your Best

The Selaron Steps in Rio de Janeiro, Brazil, are made from pieces of tile found in the city and donated from around the world.

- discuss if perfection is good.
- read about someone who changed how he did things.
- learn about an unexpected artist.
- watch a TED Talk about teaching people bravery, not perfection.
- learn how to ask for and give advice.

6A The Best I Can Be

VOCABULARY Goals and expectations

1 MY PERSPECTIVE

Look at the photo. Many of the tiles used are broken or from the trash. Do you still think the stairs are beautiful?

2 Match the words in bold with the correct definitions.

1 _____ "I have not **failed**. I've just found several thousand ways that won't work." —Thomas Edison

2 _____ "The only place where **success** comes before work is in the dictionary." —Anonymous

3 _____ "Have no fear of **perfection**; you'll never reach it." —Salvador Dali

4 _____ "Beauty is about being comfortable in your own skin. It's about knowing and **accepting** who you are." —Ellen DeGeneres

5 _____ "Practice makes **perfect**." —Anonymous

6 _____ "Practice doesn't make perfect. Practice reduces the **imperfection**." —Toba Beta

7 _____ "True success is overcoming the fear of being **unsuccessful**." —Paul Sweeney

a (n) having no mistakes or problems
b (v, past) to finish without success
c (adj) without mistakes
d (n) the correct or wanted result
e (adj) not getting the correct or wanted result
f (n) not being exactly right
g (v) to feel that something is OK or normal

3 Choose the correct options to complete the meanings of the quotations in Activity 2.

1 When you find a way that doesn't work, you learn something new. When you learn nothing, you *fail / succeed*.

2 You *don't have to / have to* work before you can succeed.

3 Perfection is a nice idea, *and we should / but we shouldn't* expect to reach it.

4 Beauty isn't about how you look; it's about *how you feel / dressing comfortably*.

5 If you want to do something really well, *you won't fail / practice a lot*.

6 You can never be perfect, *but you can / and you can't* usually improve.

7 Success means not being afraid of *other people / failure*.

4 Match the opposites. Use your dictionary if necessary.

1 perfection _____   **a** unsuccessful
2 success _____   **b** fail
3 perfect _____   **c** imperfect
4 succeed _____   **d** imperfection
5 accept _____   **e** reject
6 successful _____   **f** failure

5 Work in pairs. Discuss the questions.

1 Have you ever failed? What did you do next? Can failure lead to success?

2 Have you ever seen or experienced something that was perfect? What was it?

3 Can something be "too perfect?" Why?

LISTENING

6 Work in pairs. Discuss the questions.

1 Can you think of a food that doesn't look good but tastes delicious?
2 Have you eaten a food that looked perfect but didn't taste very good?
3 Have you ever been surprised by a food or drink? For example, something that looked sweet but tasted spicy?

7 Listen to a podcast about a fruit and vegetable seller in Tokyo. Are the sentences *true* or *false*? Rewrite the false statements. 🎧 36

1 Senbikiya is a small grocery store in Tokyo. _____
_____

2 Senbikiya isn't very successful because it's too expensive. _____
_____

3 In Japan, fruit is a popular gift because it is something you don't need. _____
_____

4 In Japan, giving fruit as a gift started recently. _____
_____

5 The carrots on this page probably don't come from Senbikiya. _____
_____

8 Listen to a podcast about a fruit and vegetable seller in France. Choose the correct options to complete the sentences. 🎧 37

1 Intermarché sells fruit and vegetables that are _____ .
   a ugly and popular　　**b** perfect but not popular　　**c** ugly and not popular

2 Customers like Intermarché's fruit and vegetables because of the _____ .
   a funny way they look　　**b** price alone　　**c** taste and price

3 In the past, most "ugly" fruit and vegetables were _____ .
   a given to animals　　**b** thrown away　　**c** sold to supermarkets

4 Rejecting imperfect fruit and vegetables _____ food.
   a wastes　　**b** lowers the price of　　**c** improves the flavor of

5 Now, _____ are choosing to eat imperfect fruit and vegetables.
   a only very hungry people　　**b** most farmers　　**c** more people

9 Work in pairs. Discuss the questions.

1 Do you think Senbikiya and Intermarché would be successful in your country? Why?
2 Which shop would you prefer: Senbikiya or Intermarché? Why?

10 CHOOSE Choose one of the following activities.

- Think of products other than food where a perfect appearance is important. Make a list of three or four things. Then think of products where an imperfect appearance is OK. Make a list of three or four things. Compare your lists with a partner.

  Perfect appearance important: *new cars,* _____

  Imperfect appearance OK: *soap,* _____

- Work in pairs. Make a list of situations when a person's appearance is important. When do people dress nicely and try to look as perfect as possible?

- Work in small groups. Think about how people present themselves on social media. Do you think people try to present themselves as more perfect and successful than they are in real life? Do you feel pressure to do this?

Look at these carrots. Do you think they still taste normal?

GRAMMAR Modals: obligation, prohibition, permission, advice

11 Answer the questions about presenting yourself online.

1 What social media sites and apps do you use?
2 What kinds of photos of yourself do you put online?
3 How do people use social media to make their lives look more interesting than they are? Do you do this?

12 Read the short article about social media. Match the words in bold with the correct meanings below. One meaning matches with two words.

Rules for the perfect profile photo?
According to the rules, you (1) **have to** be at least thirteen years old to open an account on most social media apps. Although the rules say younger kids (2) **can't** join, you (3) **don't have to** prove your age, so a lot of them still join. This worries some experts. Research shows that the "perfect lives" kids see on social media can cause them to feel bad about their own lives. Parents (4) **should** explain that what people show online isn't the whole picture. The Imperfect Tribe, a group of people that started on Instagram, agrees. They say we (5) **shouldn't** try to look perfect on social media. In fact, members of the group (6) **must** show themselves as real people online.

a It would be a good idea to do this. _____
b You are not allowed to do this. _____
c It's not necessary to do this. _____
d It's necessary for you to do this. _____
e It would be a good idea NOT to do this. _____

Modals	
Obligation: things that are necessary or not necessary to do	You **must** be thirteen or older to sign up. You **have to** choose a password. You **don't have to** pay for the service; it's free.
Prohibition: things you are not allowed to do	You **can't** wear shoes here. You **must not** wear shorts.
Permission: things that are OK to do or not necessary to do	You **can** take off your hat. You **don't have to** be quiet; you can talk.
Advice: things that would be good to do	You **should** arrive early to avoid the crowds. You **shouldn't** buy souvenirs there; they're really expensive.

Check page 138 for more information and practice.

13 Look at the Grammar box. Choose the best words to complete the quotes about school uniforms.

"We have a strict uniform policy at my school. Boys (1) *have to / can't* wear black pants, but girls (2) *shouldn't / can* choose a skirt or pants. Girls' skirts (3) *can't / must* touch the top of the knees. You (4) *can't / don't have to* loosen your tie at school during the day, and girls (5) *have to / shouldn't* let their socks fall down." —Park, Korea

"We don't have a uniform, so we (6) *can't / don't have to* wear a tie or jacket. We (7) *can / should* wear what we want, although we (8) *have to / shouldn't* come to school in beach clothes or something like that. The rules aren't specific, but they say we (9) *mustn't / should* look neat." —Sofia, Italy

14 Work in pairs. Are there rules about how to dress at your school? What advice would you give a new student about what to wear?

15 Complete the rules with the correct words.

can	can't	have to	must	should

Dressing for the temples of Thailand
Visitors to Thailand (1) _____ visit the amazing temples. But there are some rules you (2) _____ follow to be respectful. First, you (3) _____ wear shoes in the temples. Second, you (4) _____ wear clothes that cover your arms and knees. But there are no rules about covering your head. You (5) _____ enter without a hat or headscarf.

16 **PRONUNCIATION** Reduced *have to* and *has to*

Look at the Pronunciation box. Then read and listen to the conversation. Underline the reduced forms. 🎧 38

When talking about obligation, people usually don't stress *has to* and *have to* when they are in the middle of a sentence. They also usually connect the words. At the end of a sentence, or when an obligation is emphasized, *has to* and *have to* are stressed.

A Does your soccer team have to wear a suit and tie on game day?
B We don't have to, but we want to. We want to look our best.
A But everyone has to wear the official uniform to play, right?
B Yes, everyone has to. It's a rule.

17 Work in pairs. Discuss the questions.

1 When in your life have you had to wear certain clothes for a special event, job, or activity?
2 How should people dress for an important event like a college interview?

6B Finding New Ways

Not so fast

Lewis Pugh swims in Lake Imja, Mount Everest.

VOCABULARY BUILDING

Negative prefixes

A prefix can be added to the beginning of a word to change its meaning. Some prefixes give words the opposite meaning, for example:

im- (*imperfect* = not perfect)

dis- (*disagree* = not agree)

un- (*unsuccessful* = not successful)

in- (*informal* = not formal)

1 Work in pairs. Read the Vocabulary Building box. Then complete the words below with *im-*, *dis-*, *in-*, or *un-*. Use a dictionary if necessary.

Why being comfortable can be bad for your career

CEO Kathy Bloomgarden says that if you want to succeed, you need to be (1) _un_comfortable. She believes that it's (2) _____possible to grow unless you have challenges. She realized that speaking only one language was a (3) _____advantage in business, so she learned Arabic and Chinese.

Why being patient may not help you learn a new language

Blogger Benny Lewis believes that the best way to learn a language is to be (4) _____patient. If you really want to succeed, you must be (5) _____able to wait. He says that if you just start talking with people, your fear will (6) _____appear. And talking to people is an (7) _____expensive way to learn!

2 Complete the sentences so they are true for you. Share your ideas with a partner.

1 I feel *comfortable* / *uncomfortable* when…
2 For me, it would be *possible* / *impossible* to…
3 One *advantage* / *disadvantage* of the place I live is…
4 I feel *successful* / *unsuccessful* when…
5 I'm usually *able* / *unable* to…
6 Something I would like to see *appear* / *disappear* is…
7 For me, it's *perfect* / *imperfect* that…
8 I *agree* / *disagree* with…

I feel successful when I get my work done on time.

READING

3 Work with a partner. Look at the photo and the caption. Discuss the questions.

1 Where is this person? What is he doing?
2 How do you think he feels?
3 Would you ever try something like this? Why?

4 Read the article. Answer the questions.

1 Why does Lewis Pugh swim? _____
   _____
2 Where did he do a high-altitude swim? _____
   _____
3 What style of swimming was successful for him for most of his career? _____
4 What style of swimming was successful for the Lake Imja swim? _____
5 What lesson did Pugh learn through failure? _____
   _____

What are you really good at? What would you do if all of a sudden you failed at it? For "pioneer swimmer" and National Geographic Adventurer of the Year Lewis Pugh, swimming has been a way to
5 share his passion for the environment with the world. He has swum in every ocean in the world and in some dangerous places where people thought swimming would be impossible.

He swims to raise awareness for issues like global
10 warming, but the swims often take place in extremely cold temperatures. After one scary and dangerous swim at the North Pole, Lewis reached a conclusion: no more cold-water swimming.

But in 2010, he heard about the snow disappearing
15 from the Himalayas and wanted to tell the world about it. He made the decision to swim two kilometers (1.2 miles) across Lake Imja, a very cold lake near Mount Everest at 5,300 meters (17,388 feet) above sea level.

On his first attempt, he failed. Unable to breathe
20 normally at the high altitude*, he almost drowned. The experience was frightening.

However, Pugh learned something. He usually swims as fast as possible, fighting against the water. After all, don't all athletes try to be the fastest? But that was a
25 disadvantage at high altitude. Members of his team said that he must forget everything he knew about swimming and swim slowly. Instead of struggling against the water, he must stay relaxed and move easily through it.

30 Two days after his near-death experience, Pugh returned to the lake for another try. He remained calm and slowly swam across it successfully. From his failure, he learned an important lesson: If at first you don't succeed, try something different—especially when you
35 think you already know everything.

altitude *how high something is above the level of the sea*

---

5 Read the Tip. Then read the article again and match the causes with the effects.

> Readings often present causes and effects—events that lead to other situations or results. Understanding cause and effect can help you understand how the ideas in the reading are connected.

1 Pugh was afraid. _____
2 Pugh wanted people to know about global warming. _____
3 Pugh failed to swim across Lake Imja. _____
4 Pugh changed his swimming style. _____

a He went swimming near Mount Everest.
b He decided he wouldn't swim in cold water ever again.
c He succeeded in swimming across Lake Imja.
d He changed his swimming style.

6 Match the pairs of synonyms from the article.

1 fight _____   **a** scary
2 frightening _____   **b** decision
3 calm _____   **c** attempt
4 try _____   **d** struggle
5 conclusion _____   **e** relaxed

CRITICAL THINKING Making inferences

> Inference helps readers understand a meaning that isn't directly stated. For example, the article tells us that Pugh did two very difficult swims. It doesn't say directly that he's a strong swimmer, but we can make the inference that he must be a strong swimmer or he could not do those difficult swims.

7 Read the Critical Thinking box. Then choose the word in each pair of opposites that best describes Pugh's style of swimming and personality. Use your dictionary if necessary.

1 lazy   hard-working
2 confident   shy
3 successful   unsuccessful
4 afraid   brave
5 weak   strong

8 For each answer you gave in Activity 7, underline the information in the article that supports your answer.

9 Make a list of other words to describe Pugh based on what you know from the article. Use your dictionary if necessary. Share your list with a partner and discuss any differences.

6C Unexpected Art

GRAMMAR Zero conditional

1 Work in pairs. Answer the questions.

1 What do you really enjoy doing for fun?
2 Can you imagine a job that would pay you to do something you love?

2 Look at the Grammar box. Then answer the questions below.

Zero conditional	
The zero conditional with *if* and *when* is used to talk about things that are generally or always true. The result clause can include main verbs and modals.	*When you do what you love, you love what you do.* *If you don't risk failure, you can't succeed.* *When you make mistakes, you can learn a lot.*

1 In each sentence, what verb tense is used in the *if* or *when* clause?
2 What verb tense is used in the result clause of each sentence?

Check page 138 for more information and practice.

3 Complete the article with these clauses. Write the correct letter.

a you travel to New York
b you aren't stopped from painting on walls
c it doesn't feel like work
d people want to buy an artist's work
e if you work hard
f art galleries can sell it

When you love your job, (1) __c__ . That's definitely the case with street artist Lady Aiko. If (2) _____ , you may see her work on buildings—and in art galleries. Some street artists have to work in secret, but when your work is as good as Lady Aiko's, (3) _____ . In fact, you can get paid to paint on them. And if a street artist's work becomes popular, (4) _____ . When (5) _____ , the artist is doing something right.

Lady Aiko is successful because of her bravery and persistence. When she started out, most street artists were men, and people were surprised to see a woman street artist. Lady Aiko shows that (6) _____ , you can change people's expectations.

4 Look at the Grammar box. Cross out one incorrect word in each piece of advice for artists below.

Zero conditional to give advice	
The zero conditional with *if* and *when* is used with the imperative to give advice.	*If you love street art, go to Rio de Janeiro.* *When you go, visit the Selaron Steps.*
The zero conditional with *if* and *when* is also used with *should* + infinitive without *to* to give advice.	*If you visit the Selaron Steps, you should take a lot of photos.*

- If you want to be an artist, ~~should~~ do it—just start painting.
- When you aren't sure what to do, you should to just keep painting; don't stop.
- If when you want to grow as an artist, you should look at other people's work.
- When you are ready for people to see your work, if you can put your photos on the Internet.
- When you feel like you're failing, if try to learn from the experience.

5 Choose the correct options to complete the article.

Escadaria Selarón

If you (1) *go / will go* to Rio de Janeiro, Brazil, you (2) *visit / should visit* the Escadaria Selarón—the Selaron Steps. Artist Jorge Selaron started work on the steps as a hobby in 1990, but soon learned that if you (3) *love / should love* something, it can become your life's work. Before starting the steps, Selaron was a struggling painter. But soon, the steps became popular with both locals and tourists. When you first see the steps, you immediately (4) *notice / noticed* a lot of green, yellow, and blue—the colors of the Brazilian flag. According to Selaron, originally from Chile, the steps are his gift to the people of Brazil. When you (5) *can look / look closely*, you can see hundreds of words and pictures in the tiles. Selaron said that each tile tells a story. If that's true, then the stairs, made with four thousand tiles, (6) *had / have* four thousand stories to tell.

Lady Aiko painted this image in New York City, US, in 2012. She did the painting on page 74 in Dubai, UAE, in 2016.

6 **PRONUNCIATION** Conditional intonation

Read the information. Then listen and mark the upward and downward intonation on the sentences below. 🎧 40

In conditional sentences that begin with *If* or *When*, the intonation often rises on the *if/when* clause and falls on the main clause.

If you're interested in art, you should visit the Selaron Steps.

When visitors come to town, we like to show them the sights.

1 If you like street art, you should look for Lady Aiko's work.
2 When street artists become famous, they can make a lot of money.
3 If you work hard at something, your ability usually improves.
4 When you fail, try to learn from it.
5 If an artist wants a bigger audience, they can put their artwork on the Internet.
6 When you find something you love doing, you should make time for it.

7 Listen to the sentences in Activity 6 again. Then practice saying the sentences with natural conditional intonation.

8 **CHOOSE** Choose one of the following activities.

- Tourists enjoy seeing the work of Lady Aiko in New York and Jorge Selaron in Rio de Janeiro. Work in pairs. Think of things in your country that tourists enjoy seeing. Tell people to see them using zero conditional sentences. Then present your work to another pair.

- Activity 4 gives tips for street artists. Think of something you know about— learning a language, doing a sport, taking photographs—and write tips for doing it. Use zero conditional sentences.

- Jorge Selaron used broken tiles to create beauty. Think of a place in your area that isn't beautiful. Imagine how you could use recycled materials to make it beautiful. Make a poster showing your ideas and explaining the improvement. Use zero conditional sentences.

When you visit our city, you should see…

When you want to learn photography, you should start by…

When an area is ugly and dirty, people don't go there. When you make it beautiful,…

6D Teach Girls Bravery, Not Perfection

" We have to show them that they will be loved and accepted not for being perfect but for being courageous. "

RESHMA SAUJANI

Read about Reshma Saujani and get ready to watch her TED Talk. ▶ **6.0**

AUTHENTIC LISTENING SKILLS

Contrast

A **contrast** is when a speaker shows that two ideas, facts, or situations are different. Words such as *but* and *however* often mark contrasts. A speaker may also change his or her tone to mark contrast.

1 Read the Authentic Listening Skills box. Match the contrasting ideas in the excerpts from the TED Talk.

1 "She tried, she came close, but _____

2 "She'll think that her student spent the past twenty minutes just staring at the screen. But _____

3 "Girls are really good at coding, but _____

4 "We have to begin to undo the socialization of perfection, but _____

5 "This was my way to make a difference. The polls, however, _____

a if she presses 'undo' a few times, she'll see that her student wrote code and then deleted it."

b we've got to combine it with building a sisterhood* that lets girls know that they are not alone."

c it's not enough just to teach them to code."

d she didn't get it exactly right."

e told a very different story."

sisterhood *a group of girls or women who work together and help each other*

2 Listen to the excerpts and check your answers to Activity 1. 🎧 **41**

WATCH

3 Work in pairs. Discuss the questions before you watch the talk.

1 Is perfection always better or more useful than imperfection? Why?

2 Is it more important to be perfect or to try new things? Why?

3 Can always wanting to be perfect make a person not try new things? Why? Has this ever happened to you?

4 Watch Part 1 of the talk. Choose the correct options to complete the sentences. ▶ **6.1**

1 Reshma started her career working in _____ .
  a government
  b banking
  c marketing

2 She wanted to have a more active role in government to _____ .
  a make more money
  b change things
  c raise money for others

3 She tried for an elected job in government _____ .
  a and won
  b but changed her mind
  c and lost badly

4 She tells the story about running for government to show that _____ .
  a she was perfect
  b she was brave for the first time
  c she was always brave

TEDTALKS

5 Watch Part 2 of the talk. Answer the questions. ▶ 6.2

  1 What does Reshma say that boys are rewarded for, but girls are taught to avoid? _____

  2 What does she feel that girls lack?

  _____

  3 What do teachers often learn about girls who are learning to code?

  _____

  4 According to Reshma, why do girls often not answer questions? _____

  5 According to Reshma, who should teach girls to be brave?

  _____

6 **VOCABULARY IN CONTEXT**

  a Watch the clips from the TED Talk. Choose the correct meanings of the words. ▶ 6.3

  b Work in pairs. Discuss the questions.

    1 Think of a time when you had to be *courageous*. What happened?

    2 Have you ever *run* for a position, for example, captain of a sports team? What was it? What would you like to run for?

    3 What kind of things do you *negotiate* with your parents? With your teachers?

    4 Have you ever seen a person's *supportive network* in action? What was the reason?

    5 Do you think everyone has the *potential* to do something good or brave? What do you have the *potential* to do?

    6 Is there anything that you have to *struggle* with to achieve? What?

7 Think of something you have learned to do—speak a language, play a musical instrument, play a sport, or something else. Make notes.

  • What was the skill or activity?
  • What challenges did you face? How did you have to be brave to continue learning?
  • What kinds of mistakes did you make while learning it?
  • What advice would you give to someone learning the activity?

8 Work in small groups. Discuss your activity from Activity 7.

CHALLENGE

Work in groups. Discuss the questions.

1 Writing code is a process of trial and error and requires perseverance. What other activities require trial and error and perseverance?

2 Reshma says in her talk that a supportive network is an important part of learning. Have you ever had a supportive network? Who was in it?

3 Can you think of a time when you did something—even something small or simple—that felt brave? What did you learn from it?

4 The journalist Arianna Huffington said, "Failure isn't the opposite of success, it's part of success." Do you agree or disagree? Why?

5 In your country, where are girls and women underrepresented and why?

6 Reshma talks about the ways that boys are socialized. Is this also harmful to society? Does it limit the opportunities for boys? If so, how?

6E Giving Advice

SPEAKING Giving advice

1 Work in pairs. Discuss the questions.

1 Who do you usually ask for advice? Why?
2 Have you ever given advice? What about?

2 Read the question and advice. What word do you think is missing?

Q&A

SS **Sam S:** My friend is good at _____ but won't speak in class or use her _____ because she's afraid of making a mistake. She wants her _____ to be perfect. What should I say to her?

AP **Ania P:** If she wants to speak _____ , she should just start speaking _____ . Nobody notices mistakes.

SR **Sixtos R:** She should learn to love mistakes. The only way to improve is to make mistakes, especially when you have a teacher there to correct you.

RD **Ryuji D:** Why not start an _____ movie club? When you watch a movie, you naturally want to talk about it. You could have an "_____-only" rule for the club.

IM **Igor M:** I agree that she shouldn't worry about mistakes. Just keep trying. If you want to improve your _____ , try speaking it often.

Speaking strategies

Giving advice

If someone asks for advice, use these expressions.

*When you don't understand something in class, **you should** ask your teacher for help.*

*If you need more math practice, **try** downloading a math app.*

***Why don't you**…*

The best time to give advice is when someone asks for it. If someone hasn't asked, but you want to give advice, be polite and use these expressions.

*If the computer isn't working, **you might want to try** re-starting it.*

*I can see you don't have a phone signal. I got a signal near the window, and **that may work for you**.*

*I'm not sure, but **I think** this door is locked after 6:00. **You may/might** need to use the side entrance.*

3 Work in pairs. Discuss the questions.

1 Which advice do you think is the most helpful?
2 Can you think of other advice that would be useful for improving at English?
3 Have you ever received any advice for speaking English that didn't work for you?

4 Read the Speaking strategies box. Work in small groups and take turns giving advice for the situations below.

1 You can see that someone is trying to figure out where to put the coins in a drink machine. You know the correct place to put them.
2 A friend asks you what kind of phone you think they should buy.
3 You notice that someone in a store is having problems carrying their items. They probably don't realize that the store has baskets they can use.

WRITING An advice blog

5 Work in pairs. Discuss the questions.

1 How do you prepare for exams?
2 How do you feel before or during exams? Do you often feel worried or stressed?
3 What do you do to reduce your worry or stress?

6 Read the advice blog. Answer the questions.

Dealing with exam stress

It's natural to feel stressed when you have an exam. In fact, if you don't feel at least a little stressed, you probably aren't working hard enough. Stress can help make us study, but if we have too much stress, it can make us sick and reduce our chances of success. I asked my friends how they deal with exam stress. Here are their top six tips.

No one is perfect. Do your best, but remember: It won't help you to have a lot of stress and worry about getting 100 percent every time.

When you're preparing for an exam, eat well. Your brain needs food! Eat plenty of fresh fruit and vegetables.

If you feel stressed out, talk to another student about it. It helps remind you that your feelings are normal.

You may want to stay up late studying, but you should get plenty of rest. If you're too tired, you won't learn as well, and you may get sick.

Exercise is one of the best ways to fight stress and clear your mind. When you're planning your exam preparation, you should include regular physical activity.

On exam day, remember to breathe. When you breathe deeply, you feel more relaxed!

If you follow these tips, you'll improve your chances of exam success. Good luck!

1 What problem does the blog talk about? _____
2 How many solutions does the blog give? _____
3 Have you used any of these tips? If so, which ones? _____
4 Which tip do you think is the most useful? _____

7 **WRITING SKILL** Explaining problems and solutions

Read the Writing strategy box. Does the blog in Activity 6 include all of the information mentioned in the box?

8 Choose one of the problems. Ask your classmates for possible solutions.

- You are often late meeting friends, arriving at school, etc.
- You spend too much time on social media when you should be studying.
- You have too many activities—sports, music, etc. You enjoy them all, but you're too busy.

9 **WRITING SKILL** Essay structure

Write a paragraph about the problem and possible solutions. Use this structure.

1 Introduce the topic.
2 Say what the problem is.
3 Say why it's a problem.
4 Offer 3–5 solutions.
5 Give a conclusion.

10 Exchange papers with a partner. Check each other's work. Does your partner answer the questions in the Writing strategy box?

> **Writing strategy**
>
> A problem-solution paragraph usually begins with a sentence that introduces the topic. Then it answers these questions.
> - What is the problem?
> - Why is it a problem?
> - What is the solution / are the solutions?
>
> It will then often include a concluding sentence.

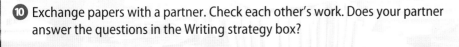

7 Tell Me What You Eat

Pad Thai is a popular dish from Thailand. It is made from noodles, shrimp or chicken, eggs, garlic, and chili pepper.

7A Food and Flavors from Around the World

VOCABULARY Foods, drinks, and flavors

1 Work in pairs. Discuss the questions.

   1 What's your favorite food? Would you like the food in the photo?
   2 Is there any food you really don't like? What is it?

2 Match each food or drink with a type and a flavor. Use your dictionary if necessary.

Foods / Drinks	Types	Flavors
chili powder	fruit	salty
lemon	vegetable	sweet
coffee	meat	sour
strawberry	spice	bitter
potato chip	drink	spicy
tomato	dessert	
chocolate	snack	
chicken		

3 Think of at least one more food or drink for each of the five flavors. Make a list.

4 Match each popular international food with the best description. Two foods do not have a description.

   1 _____ curry   **5** _____ pasta
   2 _____ french fry   **6** _____ tea
   3 _____ shrimp   **7** _____ tomato
   4 _____ ice cream   **8** _____ apple

   a Most people think of this food as Italian, but many experts think it probably came from Chinese noodles originally.
   b This is a spicy food originally from India. The strong flavor comes from the hot pepper and other spices that cooks use.
   c Many people think this red fruit is a vegetable because it is often used in salads or salty sauces. People in Mexico first grew and ate it more than 2,000 years ago.
   d Like coffee, this drink is bitter. People often add sugar to make it sweet. People in China were probably the first to drink it, but now it's popular around the world.
   e This salty food is similar to a potato chip. People eat it as a snack or with a meal. No one is sure, but it may have come from Belgium. The British call them "chips."
   f This dessert often comes in sweet fruit flavors like strawberry. It's very cold and may have come from China, but it became very popular in Italy and the UK about three hundred years ago.

5 Write descriptions like the ones in Activity 4 for a food or drink you know. Then work in pairs. Guess your partner's food.

> *This is a sweet and spicy dish. It comes from Peru. It has fish, onions, hot pepper, and lime juice.*   Ceviche?

LISTENING

6 Work in pairs. Look at the photo. Why do you think people want to grow vegetables under the sea?

7 Listen to a conversation. Match each part of the conversation with the topic. There is one extra topic. 🎧 **42**

Part 1 _____   **a** Food for the future
Part 2 _____   **b** The importance of smell
                         c Tasting what we see

8 Listen to the conversation again. Are the sentences *true* or *false*? 🎧 **42**

1 Kasia gives Marco something spicy to taste.
2 Marco tastes more with his nose closed.
3 The nose is more important than the mouth for tasting.
4 In the future, meat might come from laboratories instead of farms.
5 Scientists are growing fruit under the sea.

9 PRONUNCIATION Minimal pairs

a Sometimes, only one sound makes the difference between words, for example, *paper* and *pepper*. Listen to the sentences. Which word do you hear? 🎧 **43**

1 I need some *paper* / *pepper* for my project.
2 Can I *taste* / *toast* this bread?
3 I think green tea is *better* / *bitter*.
4 I need more *spice* / *space* for my project.
5 Did you smell the *soap* / *soup*?

b Work in pairs. Listen again. Then practice saying the sentences with both words. Can your partner tell which word you're saying? 🎧 **43**

Divers tend to an underwater basil farm in Italy.

GRAMMAR Predictions and arrangements

Predictions and arrangements

Talking about future arrangements

I'm giving my presentation next Thursday.

I'm going to give my presentation tomorrow.

Making predictions

We're going to need more food.

There will be nearly ten billion people on Earth in 2050.

We won't need as much land for farms.

We might "grow" meat in laboratories.

We might not continue raising animals for food.

We're sure this will happen.

We think this might / may happen, but we're not sure.

⑩ Look at the Grammar box. Read the sentences from the listening. Answer the questions.

1 What time period do all the sentences talk about: the present or the future?
2 Which sentences use a present tense verb form?
3 What is the shortened form of *will not*?
4 Which is more definite: *will* or *might*?
5 Which tense talks about a future arrangement?
6 Do the other sentences predict the future or talk about definite plans?

Check page 140 for more information and practice.

⑪ Choose the correct options to complete the announcement.

Science Day: Feeding a Growing Population

The science department (1) *is holding / might hold* a discussion next Monday from 3:00 to 4:00 about the future of food, and all students are invited to attend. According to science teacher Mr. Yamada, "Scientists think there (2) *will be / are being* nearly ten billion people on Earth in 2050. As the population increases, we (3) *might not / will* need more food. We (4) *are going to / won't be able to* continue raising animals for food because it uses a lot of energy." According to Yamada, this is where the science gets interesting. "To feed everyone in 2050, (5) *we might have to 'grow' / we'll 'grow'* meat in laboratories." Yamada also says that scientists are working on new ways to grow food. "Right now, researchers (6) *will experiment / are experimenting* with new ways of growing food, for example, growing crops in tunnels under the ground," he explains. "In 2050, underground farmers (7) *won't have to / aren't having to* worry so much about the weather!"

⑫ Complete each sentence. Use one verb with *going to* and one verb in the present continuous.

1 My dad ___is buying___ (buy) a 3D food printer next week because he thinks food printing ___is going to be___ (be) the next big thing.

2 We're _____ (have) dinner with our vegetarian friends next week, so I _____ (eat) vegetarian food this weekend to see what it's like.

3 Layla _____ (give) a presentation tomorrow about how future farmers _____ (grow) vegetables underwater.

4 I _____ (have) a big steak dinner tomorrow night, and I _____ (enjoy) it, because there won't be much real meat in the future!

⑬ Work in groups. Look at the list of special occasions. Pick one and plan activities and a way to celebrate. Share your plans with another group.

birthday	college acceptance	end of a sports season
good grades	graduation	wedding

It's Marcos's birthday. We're going to have a party at the park on Saturday. We're going to eat at 1 p.m.

7B The Greatest Human Success Story

VOCABULARY BUILDING

Suffixes: Verb → noun

Adding -er, -ment, or -ance to some verbs creates nouns.
-er is added to mean "a person who does something"
(work → worker). -ment is added to mean "the result of
the verb" (enjoy → enjoyment). -ance is added to mean
"a specific instance of the verb happening"
(perform → performance).

• When a verb ends in a consonant, -er can be added (worker).

• When a verb ends in b, d, f, l, m, n, p, or t, the final letter is
usually doubled (runner). Exceptions: farmer, hunter

• When a verb ends in e, add -r to make -er words.

1 Read the Vocabulary Building box. Then add a suffix
to items 1–4 to make a noun. Use your dictionary if
necessary.

People	Other nouns
1. travel – _____	2. achieve – _____
3. work – _____	4. disappear – _____
5. _____ – _____	6. _____ – _____
7. _____ – _____	

READING

2 Read the first two paragraphs of the article. Find three
more nouns that are made from verbs. Write the verb
and the noun in the table in Activity 1.

3 Read the tip. Then read the article and put letters for the
headings (a–e) next to the correct paragraph.

> Each paragraph of a text usually has a different main
> idea. By identifying the main idea of each paragraph, we
> can better understand the whole text. Usually, focusing
> on the nouns and verbs in a paragraph gives you a good
> idea of its main ideas.

a Staying in one place
b The most important workers on the farm
c Once upon a time
d Protecting our farms
e Our greatest achievement
f A long history together

4 Read the article again. Underline the information that
disagrees with each statement below.

1 The first farmers lived about five thousand years ago.
2 Plants can grow food on their own.
3 Working on farms stopped humans from making
progress in other areas.
4 Bees sometimes cause problems because they eat plants.
5 Farmers dislike bees, so they try to kill them.

5 Match the farming vocabulary from the article with the
best definition.

1 _____ agriculture   5 _____ grow
2 _____ livestock   6 _____ harvest
3 _____ community   7 _____ plant
4 _____ crop   8 _____ season

a animals raised for meat
b a food plant
c to collect food from plants
d farming
e part of the year
f to put a plant into the ground
g to give a plant what it needs to develop
h a group of people who live or work together or who have
something in common

6 Do the following. Use your dictionary if necessary.

1 Name two types of livestock.
2 Name two crops that grow in your country.
3 Put these words in the order that farmers do them:
harvest, plant, grow.
4 Name two or three places in your region or country
where there are a lot of farms.

7 Work in pairs. Cover the article. Tell each other what you
have learned about:

• how agriculture changed the lives of humans.
• why bees are important.
• why bees may be disappearing.

8 CHOOSE

Read the labels on the picture. Do one of the following.

• Discuss in pairs. What foods have you eaten recently that
would be gone if bees disappeared?

• Write a shopping list for a dinner party. All dishes must
use food that's pollinated by bees.

• Use the Internet to find more information about the
decreasing bee population. Write a list of things that
people can do to help.

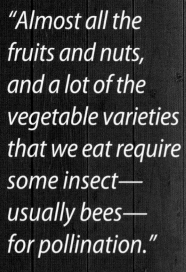

> *"Almost all the fruits and nuts, and a lot of the vegetable varieties that we eat require some insect— usually bees— for pollination."*
>
> SAM DROEGE, BEE EXPERT

PB & J
No jelly or peanut butter

No salsa

No guacamole
(no avocados)

Pasta salad
Pasta is OK, but no broccoli, olives, onions, peppers, or tomatoes

Blackberry pie
No berries

Greek salad
No tomatoes, cucumbers, onions, or olives. Feta cheese is OK, but too salty without the vegetables!

Fruit salad
Banana and pineapple only. No strawberries, grapes, blueberries, or kiwi.

Lemonade
No lemons, so it's just sugar and water. Too sweet!

Kabobs
Meat is OK, but no onions, peppers, or tomatoes

The Most Important Farmers

🎧 **44** _____ Before the first farms appeared, humans were hunters, following animals and the seasons from place to place. Along with the meat they killed, they ate fruit, vegetables, and nuts that they found as they traveled.
5 And then, in different places all over the world, people began farming. This happened at least 10,000 years ago.

_____ One requirement of farming is that people stay in one place. Farmers need time to plant crops in the spring, care for them through the summer, and harvest them in
10 the fall. Livestock that are raised for meat need to stay where there is a good supply of food and water.

_____ This required people to work together as a community: some farmed, some tended to the livestock, some built houses or cooked. Farmers had to work hard
15 to keep everyone fed, but none of this would have been possible without one creature: bees. These hardworking insects transfer pollen from plant to plant. This causes healthy plants to produce fruit and vegetables, both on farms and in nature. Without bees, most plants can't make
20 the things people eat—from apples to corn to tomatoes. Eventually, people began keeping bees in order to help with crops as well as provide honey.

_____ Experts believe that bees were domesticated 4,500 years ago in Egypt. This allowed for more crops and
25 bigger cities and towns to grow. As villages and towns grew, people built more and more houses to live in and buildings to store food. Bees come in handy here, too. Experts think that containers made from beeswax started being used for storage at least 9,000 years ago.

30 _____ We've been to the moon, but agriculture is probably the biggest human success story. You may not think about it often, but almost everything you eat every day is a product of farming. By growing our food rather than finding it or hunting for it, we have allowed
35 ourselves to think new thoughts and make new things. We have turned our villages into towns and our towns into great cities and created the modern world. Without bees, none of this would have been possible.

_____ Recently, the number of bees has dropped. Why?
40 Some insects eat plants, so farmers use chemicals to kill these insects. But this also can kill bees. We now know that the disappearance of bees around the world is an increasing problem and these chemicals are one of the causes. If we keep losing bees, we may soon have difficulty
45 growing food. Some experts believe that if farmers continue using chemicals, the bee population will continue to fall. Fortunately, farmers are beginning to understand the situation and are finding safer ways to fight the insects that cause problems. Farming will continue to be our greatest
50 success story only if we protect the bees.

The countryside near Kars, Turkey

7C A Taste of Honey

GRAMMAR First conditional

First conditional

Use the first conditional to talk about possible future situations.

If we protect the bees, farming will continue to be our greatest success story.

If we continue to lose bees, we may soon have difficulty growing food.

If farmers continue using chemicals, the bee population might continue to fall.

Bees will return only when we stop using dangerous chemicals.

1 Look at the Grammar box and answer the questions.

   1 Are the actions in the result clauses possible or not? _____
   2 What tense is used for the *if* or *when* clause? _____
   3 What tense is used in the result clause? _____
   4 Which is more certain, *if* or *when*? _____

   Check page 140 for more information and practice.

2 Put the phrases in the best place to complete the text below.

   The Balyolu—Turkey's Honey Road
   If you go walking in the countryside near the Turkish city of Kars,
   (1) ____d____—or several. For centuries, the local people have raised bees for
   the honey they make. And you'll certainly have a chance to taste some if
   (2) _____ . If you taste carefully, (3) _____ as you move along the trail.
   But watch out! If (4) _____ , you could ruin your trip with a stomachache!

   a you walk the Honey Road
   b you eat too much honey
   c you may notice the changing flavors in the honey
   d you might meet a beekeeper*

   beekeeper *a person who takes care of bees and gathers their honey*

3 Choose the best words to complete the article.

   Saving food traditions for the future
   The Honey Road was the idea of National Geographic Explorer Catherine Jaffee.
   Why is honey important to her? All over the world, young people are moving
   from rural areas to cities. If they (1) *leave / will leave* their villages, they
   (2) *didn't / won't* continue to learn about their own local foods and food
   traditions—like beekeeping. She believes that if we (3) *don't / will* keep
   traditions like beekeeping alive, (4) *we / we may* lose them forever—and lose
   part of who we are. Thanks to efforts like this, (5) *will / when* future generations
   look back, (6) *they will / they* thank us for keeping foods and traditions alive.

4 Choose *if* or *when* to complete the exchanges.

   1 A Are you coming to Kars next month?
      B Yes. *When / If* I get there, I'll call you.

   2 A It may rain tomorrow.
      B *When / If* it rains, the bees won't be active.

   3 A We have one more hour to work on our project today.
      B *When / If* we work quickly, we may finish it.

4 A I have an appointment with Mr. Sato tomorrow.

B *When / If* you see him, say hello for me.

5 Listen to the exchanges and check your answers to Activity 4. 🎧 **45**

6 Work in pairs. Write your own endings to the sentences. Use *will, may, could,* and *might* at least once each.

1 If I get hungry before the end of school today, I _____ .

2 When I have dinner tonight, I *'ll eat...*_____ .

3 If my friends and I have lunch together next week, we _____ .

4 When I get home from school today, I _____ .

5 If we go to a restaurant for my next birthday, we _____ .

7 Work in groups. Discuss what you have learned in this unit by making "conditional chains." Talk about:

- *If we protect bees,...*
- *If we grow vegetables underwater,...*
- *If people leave rural areas to live in cities,...*

protect bees ⟶ no pollen problem ⟶ plants grow well ⟶ plants make food ⟶ people have enough food for the future

A *If we protect bees, there will be no pollen problem.*

B *If there is no pollen problem, plants will grow well.*

C *If plants grow well, they'll make food.*

8 CHOOSE

Choose one of the following activities.

- Work in pairs. Pick one of the issues in Activity 7. Discuss what people can do at each part of the chain to help the situation.

- Write a paragraph using one of the chains as a model.

- Work in groups. Think of a new issue to make a conditional chain for. Present your ideas to the class.

A beekeeper in Turkey collects honey—one of the world's most ancient foods.

7D The Global Food Waste Scandal

> ❝ The best thing to do with food is to eat and enjoy it, and to stop wasting it. ❞
>
> **TRISTRAM STUART**

Read about Tristram Stuart and get ready to watch his TED Talk. ▶ **7.0**

AUTHENTIC LISTENING SKILLS

Prediction

Sometimes you can use what you already know about a topic to predict what a speaker might say. This can help you understand more of what you hear.

1 Read the Authentic Listening Skills box. Based on the title of the talk and the quote above, what do you think Tristram Stuart is likely to talk about? Check (√) the topics you think he may discuss.

- ☐ Hunger isn't a big problem in rich countries.
- ☐ Cooking is a useful skill.
- ☐ Fast food often isn't very tasty.
- ☐ The biggest problem isn't too little food, but too much.
- ☐ We need to stop wasting food.
- ☐ We can save money by eating less.

2 Listen to an extract from the talk and check your answers to Activity 1. 🎧 **46**

WATCH

3 Watch Part 1 of the talk. Choose the correct option. ▶ **7.1**

1 People started trying to create a food surplus _____ years ago.

   a 1,200   **b** 12,000   **c** 120,000

2 Now, our agriculture cuts too many trees, uses too much _____ , and pollutes the air.

   a space   **b** gas   **c** water

3 Stuart found a package of biscuits (cookies) in the garbage behind a _____ .

   a supermarket   **b** restaurant   **c** house

4 Watch Part 2 of the talk. Write the correct numbers to complete the pie chart. ▶ **7.2**

Food use and waste

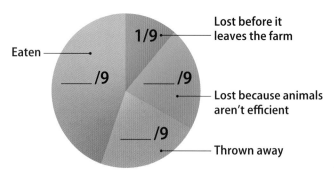

5 Watch Part 3 of the talk. Answer the questions. ▶ **7.3**

1 Stuart shows a picture of thrown away packaged food. Where was it thrown away? _____

2 How many slices of bread did the factory throw away each day? _____

3 The farmer had to throw away the spinach crop because something was growing with it. What was it? _____

TEDTALKS

6 Watch Part 4 of the talk. Choose the correct option.
▶ 7.4

1 Stuart says we need to tell *friends and neighbors / corporations and governments* to stop food waste.
2 He says we should store lettuce in *the fridge / a vase of water.*
3 Stuart *fed "waste" food to / collected "waste food" from* 5,000 people.

7 VOCABULARY IN CONTEXT

a Watch the clips from the talk. Choose the correct meaning of the words or phrases. ▶ 7.5
b Complete the sentences with your own words. Discuss your answers with a partner.

1 _____ is a *global* challenge.
2 The people who live in my *household* are
    _____ .
3 The government should *invest* more money in
    _____ .
4 A *resource* I can help conserve (keep safe) is
    _____ .
5 A problem that needs to be *tackled* in my community
    is _____ .

CRITICAL THINKING Supporting evidence

When people present an idea, they often give examples
to support their idea. This makes the idea more believable.

8 Match Stuart's ideas with the examples that support them.

1 _____ Supermarkets waste food.
2 _____ The sandwich industry wastes bread.
3 _____ Cosmetic standards cause food waste.
4 _____ We can store food in a better way.

a A photo of discarded bread crusts
b Photos of lettuce stored correctly and incorrectly
c A photo of packaged foods on a shelf
d Photos of piles of wasted parsnips, oranges, and bananas

9 Work in pairs. Discuss the questions.

1 Who do you think sets cosmetic standards for food?
2 Are cosmetic standards for food important to you personally? Why?
3 Do you see food waste at your school? What could be done to reduce it?

CHALLENGE

Which of the ideas from Stuart's talk could you or
would you try? Tell your partner and explain your
reasons.

- Eating sandwiches made with the ends of a loaf of bread
- Eating safe, fresh food that the supermarket has thrown away
- Eating fruit or vegetables that don't look perfect
- Organizing campaigns to get companies or governments to reduce food waste
- Organizing an event to celebrate food

7E What's it like?

Useful language

Making suggestions

How about…

I think we should have…

We could cook…

Why don't we (ask people to bring)…

Maybe we should…

What about…

Describing food

It's a kind of…

It's popular in…

It's really good with…

It's a little salty / fairly sweet / kind of sour / delicious.

Making decisions

We'll have plenty of pizza and the salad.

I'll put that on the invitation.

SPEAKING Planning a meal

1 Look at the photo. Answer the questions.

  1 What foods can you see in the picture?

  2 Are there foods there that you wouldn't eat? Why not?

  3 What foods would you choose for an informal party with your friends?

2 Look at the Useful language box. Then listen to the conversation. What are the people planning? Check the expressions from the Useful language box you hear. 🎧 **47**

3 Listen again. Make notes about the food they're planning to eat. 🎧 **47**

4 Imagine you're planning a meal for a party with your class. What foods and drinks would you like to include? Make notes.

5 Work in small groups. Imagine you're planning a meal for your class. Use your notes from Activity 4. Make suggestions of foods and practice describing them. Use expressions from the Useful language box.

WRITING A restaurant review

6 Answer the questions.

  1 What kinds of restaurants does your town or city have?

  2 What is the most popular type of casual food in your area? Do you like this food?

  3 What restaurant would you go to with a visitor to your town or city? Why?

All over the world, people love to eat together and share food with friends.

7 Read the Writing strategy box. Then match each question in the box with the information in the review below.

Brasserie Baron, Paris

- _____ Place Auguste Baron

- _____ Friday and Saturday, 7:30–11:00 p.m. Sunday and Monday, 7:30–10:30 p.m.

- _____ Relaxing, comfortable, welcoming.

- _____ Brasserie Baron is a zero-waste restaurant. This means that they often prepare their meals with "imperfect" fruit and vegetables and donate any remaining food. The food is prepared by professional chefs who know how to prepare "tired" ingredients safely.

- _____ Not at all. A tasty meal costs about ten euros— very cheap for Paris.

- _____ Very good—super friendly.

- _____ Yes. It's a great night out.

8 **WRITING SKILL** Describing a place

Work in small groups. Think of two or three restaurants or eating areas. Discuss where they're located, when they're open, what the atmosphere is like, and what kind of food they have.

9 Choose one place from Activity 8 and write a description of it. Answer the questions from the Writing strategy box.

10 Exchange texts with a partner. Check each other's work. Does it answer the questions from the Writing strategy box?

8 Buyer's Choice

A woman shops for shoes at a mall in Hefei, China.

IN THIS UNIT, YOU...

- talk about why we buy things and how they get to us.

- read about a company that's saving the surf.

- learn about making new products from old ones.

- watch a TED Talk about saving an island paradise.

- persuade people to make a change.

8A Why We Buy

VOCABULARY A product's life

1 Work in pairs. Discuss the questions.

1 What kinds of things do you buy for yourself? Clothes? Music? Books? Other things?
2 Where do you like to shop? Online? In stores? At markets or shopping malls? In department stores?
3 Look at the photo. What would you do if you had this many options? How would you choose what to buy? What would be important to you (price, color, style, etc.)?

2 Complete the sentences with the correct words.

| advertises | design | grows | manufacture | ~~material~~ |
| pick | produce | recycle | sell | throw ~~away~~ |

1 The _material_ is made from wool and cotton.
2 The company _____ online and on TV.
3 He will _____ the bottles, not _____ them _away_ .
4 The artist drew a good _____ for the new product.
5 Farmworkers _____ the fruit after it _____ .
6 Machines are used to _____ the goods. Machines can _____ faster than people can.
7 She is going to _____ her goods at the market.

3 Choose the correct options to complete the sentences about a clothing company called Kuyichi.

1 *Designs* / *Recycles* really cool clothes.
2 Pays a fair price for cotton from the people who *grow* / *manufacture* it.
3 Also uses cotton *picked* / *recycled* from old clothes.
4 Uses factories in Tunisia, Turkey, China, India, and Macedonia to *sell* / *manufacture* the clothes.
5 *Produces* / *Advertises* with phrases such as "pure goods."
6 *Sells* / *Picks* their clothes through their online store.
7 Asks customers not to *throw away* / *recycle* old clothes.
8 Wants customers to *throw away* / *recycle* old clothes or give them to charity.

4 MY PERSPECTIVE

Look at the information in Activity 3. Work in pairs. Discuss the questions.

1 Kuyichi's advertisements say they are doing good in the world. Do you agree that they are? Why?
2 Does doing good things for the world, like recycling, help sell products?
3 What advertisements have you seen recently? What did they say or show?
4 Did the ads make you want to buy something? Why?

5 How do the choices you make when shopping affect these things?

• your wallet
• the environment
• your self-esteem
• your community

LISTENING

6 Look at the infographic. Match the steps in the life of a shirt (1–6) with the labels below.

a __3__ **design** and **produce** the shirt
b ____ **advertise** and **sell** it
c ____ **grow** and **pick** cotton
d ____ **throw** it **away** or **recycle** it
e ____ **manufacture** the cotton **material**
f ____ **deliver** the shirt to stores

7 Listen to a fashion podcast about Kuyichi clothes. Number the topics in the order Pietro and Agata talk about them. 🎧 48

a ____ Cotton recycling
b ____ The design of the clothes
c ____ Cotton growers
d ____ Where you can buy them
e ____ Producing Kuyichi clothes
f ____ Reducing waste and pollution
g ____ Advertisements

8 Listen to the podcast again. Choose the correct option to complete each sentence. 🎧 48

1 Kuyichi is a company from *the Netherlands* / *Japan*.
2 Some of their advertisements say, "*love fashion.*" / "*love the world.*"
3 Some of their cotton growers are in *Turkey* / *Brazil*.
4 They use recycled materials to reduce *price* / *waste*.
5 Pietro wears Kuyichi clothes because they *fit well* / *look good*.
6 Kuyichi makes some of its clothes in *China* / *Thailand*.
7 Pietro says that buying online is the *cheapest* / *easiest* way.
8 Kuyichi *wants* / *doesn't want* their clothes to go to charity.

GRAMMAR Second conditional

9 Read these sentences from the podcast. Choose the correct option to complete each sentence. Then read the information below.

> ### Second conditional
>
> *If more companies were like Kuyichi, the world would be a better place.*
> *If they didn't look good, I wouldn't wear them.*
>
> 1 There *are / aren't* a lot of companies like Kuyichi.
> 2 The world *is / isn't* a better place.
> 3 Kuyichi's clothes *look / don't look* good.
> 4 The speaker *does / doesn't* wear Kuyichi clothes.
> 5 The *If* clause of both sentences talks about *the past / a situation that isn't real*.
>
> The second conditional is used to talk about situations that are imaginary, untrue, or very unlikely:
> *If advertising were stopped all over the world, companies would lose money.*
> *If Times Square in New York didn't have billboards, it would be really boring.*

10 Put the words in the correct order to make sentences.

1 sell anything / we wouldn't / If we / advertise, / didn't

_____ .

2 your old clothes, / If you didn't / you could / throw away / recycle them

_____ .

3 grow cotton / They would / didn't grow corn / if they

_____ .

4 would sell / The store / if it were / more things / bigger

_____ .

5 a coat, / you could / If / make it / I designed

_____ .

6 online / sold them / We could / for less if / sell our products / we

_____ .

Check page 142 for more information and practice.

11 Match the sentence halves. Then say whether each sentence is first conditional or second conditional. If necessary, check the Grammar Reference to review the first conditional.

1 If companies pay workers well, _____
2 If companies don't advertise, _____
3 If billboards were beautiful, _____
4 If companies didn't advertise, _____
5 If customers like an advertisement, _____

a people won't know about their products.
b people wouldn't know about their products.
c people wouldn't want to remove them.
d they will buy a product.
e they will be happy.

12 Choose the correct options to complete the article about advertisements in cities.

The mayor of Sao Paulo, Brazil, wanted to make his city a better place, so he signed a law banning billboards. He called outdoor advertisements a type of pollution. Other cities have now done the same thing. If you go to Chennai in India, (1) *you'll / you would* notice a difference from other big cities in India since a 2009 law ended outdoor advertising. And you won't see any billboards if you (2) *will walk / walk* down the streets of Grenoble, France, either. Tehran, Iran, replaced 1,500 billboards with art for ten days. The change was popular, and many people (3) *will / would* be happy if it happened again. But not every city is ready to stop advertising. If you (4) *took / take* the famous billboards away from New York's Times Square, you'd ruin one of the city's most famous tourist attractions. And would people visit Piccadilly Circus in London if its famous advertisements (5) *aren't / weren't* there?

13 Work in pairs. Discuss the questions. Take notes. Remember to use the second conditional.

1 If you were able to change your town or city to make it a better place, how would you change it?
2 If your town had no advertising, how would it be different?
3 How would people in your town feel if advertising were stopped?

14 MY PERSPECTIVE

Work in small groups. Using the ideas you discussed in Activity 13, prepare a presentation about why you think billboards should or shouldn't be allowed in your city.

8B Saving the Surf

VOCABULARY BUILDING

Compound nouns

Compound nouns can be:

- two words joined to make one word, like *billboard*
- two words used together to name one thing, but not joined, like *tourist attraction*

The first word always tells us something about the second. For example, a *billboard* is a type of *board*, not a type of *bill*.

1 Read the Vocabulary Building box. Then match the words to make compound nouns. Use your dictionary if necessary.

1	shopping _____	**a**	pollution
2	air _____	**b**	forests
3	sea _____	**c**	bags
4	rain _____	**d**	program
5	recycling _____	**e**	life

2 **PRONUNCIATION** Compound noun stress

Listen to the words. Notice the stress. Practice saying them with a partner. 🎧 49

3 Complete the sentences with the compound nouns from Activity 1.

1 Many supermarkets make shoppers pay for plastic
_____ .

2 Plastic bags can end up in the ocean and hurt
_____ .

3 Electric cars will help to reduce _____ .

4 In most countries, selling new wood products that come from _____ is not allowed.

5 The Body Shop was one of the first stores to have a _____ for customers to return empty bottles.

READING

4 Work in pairs. Look at the compound nouns from the article. What do you think they mean? What kind of company do you think the article is about?

fishnet   skateboard   fishing boat   fishermen   surfboard

5 Read the article. Choose the correct option to complete each sentence.

1 Kneppers and Stover enjoy *surfing* / *fishing*.
2 They were unhappy about *garbage* / *fishing boats* in the water.
3 Their company produces *fishnets* / *skateboards*.

4 They collect materials from *fishermen* / *the sea*.
5 Their customers *don't care* / *love* where the skateboards come from.
6 The first skateboards appeared in *Paris* / *Chile*.

6 Read the article again. Answer the questions.

1 What did Kneppers and Stover find in the ocean?
2 Who is Kevin Ahearn?
3 Where does the name of their company come from?
4 Why do fishermen throw their old nets into the sea?
5 In which countries can you find a Bureo board in a shop?

7 Read the tip. Then read the first paragraph of the article. Say what each pronoun refers to.

In a text, pronouns such as *this, that, these, those, they, them, he, she,* and *it* refer to other things in the text. For example, I have a **new skateboard**. **It** was made in Chile. Understanding these connections across sentences will help you understand the text.

1 Line 2: *they*
  a their surfboards   **b** Ben and Dave   **c** the waves
2 Line 6: *this*
  a surfing   **b** the waves   **c** trash
3 Line 8: *its*
  a the world   **b** action   **c** a friend
4 Line 16: *it*
  a Santiago, Chile   **b** Bureo   **c** a skateboard

CRITICAL THINKING Identifying supporting information

8 Underline the supporting information in the sentences.

Writers can add specific information to make their text clearer and more interesting to read. Supporting information shows why certain facts are true or important.

1 They often find lots of trash—plastic bags, bottles, and boxes—and old fishnets.
2 They started a business in Chile, one of their favorite surfing destinations.
3 They named their company Bureo, which means *the waves* in a native Chilean language.

9 Match the sentences in Activity 8 with a reason (a–c) why the extra information was given.

a Says why someone made a certain choice _____
b Explains the meaning of an unfamiliar word _____
c Gives specific examples of a more general word _____

Saving the Surf

🎧 **50** Ben Kneppers and Dave Stover love the ocean. And they love it most of all when they're on their surfboards. For them, there's nothing better than a day out on the waves. Unfortunately, when they go surfing,
5 they often find lots of trash—plastic bags, bottles, and boxes—and also old fishnets. And of course this makes them unhappy. But they know that if you just complain, the world won't change on its own, so they decided to take action. Ben and
10 Dave got together with a friend who also loves the ocean and surfing— Kevin Ahearn. They started a business in Chile, one of their favorite surfing destinations. They named their company
15 Bureo, which means *the waves* in a native Chilean language, and it designs, produces, and sells skateboards.

What's the connection between skateboards and plastic garbage in the
20 ocean? Fishnets are made of plastic. When workers on fishing boats need to throw away old or damaged nets, they usually just drop them into the sea.

It's easy to do, and there's no easy way to get rid of them—until now. Bureo has set up a fishnet recycling
25 program that makes it easy to get rid of old nets. Instead of throwing them out of the boat and into the water, fishermen can leave their old nets at Bureo's recycling centers. This is almost as easy as throwing them into the sea, and the local fishermen are happy to help clean
30 up the ocean. Bureo has a factory in Chile which turns the old nets into plastic material to make skateboards. If Bureo wasn't doing this work, tons of old fishnets would end up in the water as pollution.
35 The company turns plastic garbage into something people want to buy.

Bureo sells its boards over the Internet and also delivers them to shops in the US, Chile, Japan, and Switzerland. Skaters
40 everywhere love them not only because they're great skateboards, but also because they know that Bureo is cleaning up the ocean, one old fishnet at a time.

WHO INVENTED SKATEBOARDS?

The first skateboards appeared in the 1940s, probably in Paris. A woman named Betty Magnuson reported seeing French children riding them in 1944, when she was working there. They made them by putting wheels on the bottom of old pieces of wood.

One of Bureo's skateboards on top of the kind of fishnet it is made out of.

8C New Things from Old Ones

GRAMMAR Defining relative clauses

1 Read the extract from the article about Bureo. Answer the questions.

> ### Defining relative clauses
>
> *They got together with a friend **who** also loves the ocean and surfing—Kevin Ahearn. Bureo has set up a fishnet recycling program **that** makes it easy to get rid of old nets. Bureo has a factory in Chile **which** turns the old nets into plastic material to make skateboards.*
>
> **1** In each sentence, what noun does the pronoun in bold refer to?
>
> who: _____   that: _____   which: _____
>
> **2** What do the words after *that*, *who*, and *which* introduce?
> - The pronouns *that*, *who*, and *which* introduce more information about the nouns that come *before* / *after* them.
> - The information that comes after the relative pronouns *that*, *who*, and *which* is *important* / *not important* to the meaning of the sentence.
>
> Defining relative clauses explain which person or thing is being talked about. If you remove a defining relative clause, the meaning of the sentence changes. Defining relative clauses are introduced by *who* for people, and *which* or *that* for people or things.
>
> A relative pronoun is not needed when it is the object of the relative clause:
> *This is the chair that broke. This is the chair (that) I made.*

2 Put the defining relative clauses in the correct places to complete the sentences.

1 Artijulos is a home-furnishings store __b__ in Madrid. These are things _____ — for example, a vase— _____ .

   a that used to be other things   **b** that specializes in "upcycled" products
   c that used to be a light bulb

2 Asher Jay is a designer _____ . She brings attention to global issues _____ , including environmental and human-rights issues.

   a that need solutions   **b** who creates art and advertising

3 Local First is an organization _____ to buy from businesses _____ in the same area where they're sold.

   a that make their products   **b** that encourages consumers

4 Arthur Huang is an engineer _____ . When his company designed and built a store for Nike, he used materials _____ .

   a who believes in using recycled products
   b that were made from old bottles, cans, and DVDs

Check page 142 for more information and practice.

French artist Paulo Grangeon makes pandas out of recycled paper. He shows the pandas at famous landmarks around the world.

3 Read the article. Cross out the relative pronouns where possible.

Shopping for clothes to upcycle

Every year, about ten billion kilograms of old clothes and material (1) **that** no one wants end up in the trash. Erica Domesek, the fashion designer (2) **who** started the popular website psimadethis.com, wants to change that. She shows people (3) **who** want to dress in an original, interesting way how to upcycle old clothes. You can use old clothes (4) **that** you no longer wear or cheap clothes (5) **which** come from thrift stores*. If you're someone (6) **who** loves shopping, the thrift store option is a good one. You get the pleasure (7) **that** comes from shopping without the pain of spending a lot of money. In one video, Erica shows how you can choose a T-shirt in a color (8) **that** you really like and turn it into a fashionable scarf.

thrift store *a store that sells second-hand clothes*

4 Complete each sentence with *who*, *that*, or *which* where necessary.

1 This is the shirt _____ I made.
2 Shopping isn't an activity _____ interests me.
3 I have a cousin _____ always gives me her old clothes.
4 This is the old leather jacket _____ I bought from my friend.
5 That's the store _____ we like because the clothes aren't expensive.
6 She's the friend _____ went shopping with me last week.

5 Look at the list of words associated with stores and shopping. Use sentences with defining relative clauses to say what each thing is. Use your dictionary if necessary.

cash	checkout
clothes store	credit card
customer	furniture store
online store	salesperson
second-hand store	security guard
shopping mall	supermarket

A customer is a person who buys something in a store.

6 CHOOSE

Choose one of the following activities.

* Use the Internet to find photos of upcycled products. Write sentences that describe them. Use defining relative clauses. Share your ideas with the class.

* Pick three places where you like to shop. Write definitions for each using relative clauses. See if a partner can guess each place.

* Find out about another product like Bureo skateboards that comes from either recycled plastic or metal. Make a poster explaining how the recycling process works.

This table was upcycled from an old tractor.

" Go for it! Make that difference! "

MELATI AND ISABEL WIJSEN

Read about Melati and Isabel Wijsen and get ready to watch their TED Talk. ▶ 8.0

AUTHENTIC LISTENING SKILLS

Content words

When you listen to authentic speech, you may not understand every word. However, the most important words—usually nouns and verbs—are often stressed. Listen for the stressed words and use them to figure out the meaning of what someone is saying.

1 Read the Authentic Listening Skills box. Then listen to part of the TED Talk. What do you notice about the underlined words? Practice saying the sentences with a partner. 🎧 51

In Bali, we generate <u>680 cubic meters</u> of <u>plastic garbage a day</u>. That's about a <u>fourteen-story building</u>. And when it comes to <u>plastic bags</u>, less than <u>five percent</u> gets <u>recycled</u>.

2 Listen to another part of the talk. Complete it with the content words you hear. 🎧 52

We know that changes the image you may have of our (1) _____ . It changed ours, too, when we learned about it, when we learned that almost (2) _____ plastic bags in (3) _____ end up in our drains and then in our (4) _____ and then in our (5) _____ . And those that don't even make it to the ocean, they're either (6) _____ or littered.

WATCH

3 Work in pairs. Have you ever thought something going on at your school or home was wrong? Did you do anything about it? What other things could you have done to change the situation?

4 Watch Part 1 of the talk. Complete the notes. ▶ 8.1

Two images of Bali: Island of gods and island of (1) _____

Problem: most plastic bags aren't (2) _____ and end up in the ocean

Solution: say (3) _____ to plastic bags
Melati and Isabel: (4) _____ by Mahatma Gandhi to go on a (5) _____ strike

5 Watch Part 2 of the talk. Choose the correct option to complete each sentence. ▶ 8.2

1 The governor of Bali agreed to *meet / talk on the phone with* the girls.
2 The governor *didn't promise / promised* to help them with their campaign.
3 Their campaign: for *stores and restaurants / beaches* to become "bag-free" zones
4 They believe that *kids / only governments* have the power to change the world.
5 They want to stop people *in shops / at the airport* and ask about their plastic bags.

6 VOCABULARY IN CONTEXT

a Watch the clips from the talk. Choose the correct meanings of the words and phrases. ▶ 8.3

b Complete the sentences so they are true for you.

1 Thinking of problems in the world, I'd like to do something about _____ .

2 An example of a person who walks his or her talk is _____ .

3 An example of a person who has made a difference in my life is _____ .

4 A time in my life when I went for it was when I _____ .

5 A person who is a good example for others and tries to be the change they want in the world is _____ .

CRITICAL THINKING Understanding a speaker's authority

When you think about a speaker's message, consider their experience. When a speaker talks about things they have actually done, their argument is stronger. They have more authority.

7 Isabel and Melati tell us to "Go for it!" and to "Make that difference." What is the best reason why we should listen to them?

a They have watched other people successfully make changes in the world.

b They know that a lot of people believe that plastic bags are a serious problem.

c They've actually done what they're telling us to do, and they've succeeded.

CHALLENGE

Work in small groups. Isabel and Melati chose to make a positive change in their area. What could you and your friends do to make your world a better place? Think about the following:

- where you shop
- the things you buy
- how products are packaged
- what you do with things you no longer use

Take notes about your ideas.

8 Work in the same group. Plan a campaign like the one the Wijsen sisters started. Use your ideas from CHALLENGE. Think about how you will start the campaign, what you will do, who will help you, and how you will get more support. Present your ideas to the class.

8E Call to Action

SPEAKING How to persuade

1 Work in pairs. Answer the questions.

1 Some shopping areas have pedestrian zones—areas that are closed to cars. Does your town or city have any pedestrian zones?
2 What are the benefits of having shopping areas with no cars?
3 What problems can be caused by closing roads?

2 Listen to the presentation. Choose the correct options to complete the paragraph. What is the speaker trying to persuade the audience to do? 🎧 **53**

We want to ban (1) *cars / buses and trucks* from Fourth Avenue. Downtown (2) *entertainment / shopping* is an important part of the local economy. Research shows that people enjoy (3) *walking / eating outdoors* but don't like traffic or air pollution. A pleasant downtown area for (4) *families / teenagers* will mean a happier town. Allowing cars to ruin the (5) *shopping area / air* is wrong—people have a right to (6) *shop / feel safe*.

3 Read the Speaking strategies box. Write the strategy that matches each quotation.

_____ Closing roads to traffic is the right thing to do. Allowing cars to spoil our shopping area is wrong.

_____ Think especially of families who have young children. They just want a nice place to go shopping.

_____ Research shows that people who shop downtown enjoy walking but don't like the car and bus traffic.

4 Read the situations. In each case, how would you persuade people in your town to make a change? Brainstorm ideas as a class.

- People throw away a lot of metal, paper, and plastic instead of recycling it.
- The city wants to build a mall, but people think it will hurt local shops.
- A lot of old clothes end up in the trash. There should be a good way to exchange, reuse, and upcycle clothes.

5 Work in small groups. Choose an idea from Activity 4. Make a presentation persuading your audience to make a change. Use each of the three strategies in the box.

Speaking strategies

How to persuade

Use logic:

Research shows that… , Science has proven that… , If… , then…

Use emotion:

Think of… , How would you feel if… , My heart tells me that…

Use morals (right and wrong):

… is the right thing to do, It's wrong to…

People shop for flowers in a shopping area in Barcelona, Spain.

WRITING   A persuasive blog post

6 Work in pairs. Answer the questions.

1 Do you have performers in the shopping areas of your town or city? What kinds?
2 Do you think performers should be allowed in busy shopping areas? Why?

7 Read the blog post. Answer the questions.

Making music shouldn't be a crime

When I went to Paris, I enjoyed the performers who played music, did tricks, or painted pictures on the sidewalk. My town doesn't allow street performers. We should change that.

The world's great cities have street performers: Tokyo, Edinburgh, Barcelona, Mexico City. If we allowed them here, people would come to watch them and would also shop. This would help the local economy.

How did you feel the last time you saw a great street performer? They make a connection with the audience, and they make visitors feel welcome.

Some people earn their living this way. It's wrong to stop people from doing honest work. It would be right to change the rules to allow street performers.

If we allowed them, it would improve our quality of life and give entertainers opportunities to perform. Please click on this link to join my campaign.

1 What did the blogger love about Paris?
2 How does the blogger want to change the downtown shopping area?
3 How does the blogger use logic?
4 How does the blogger use emotion?
5 How does the blogger use ideas of right and wrong?
6 Does the blog persuade you? Why?

8 Read the Writing strategy box. Match the points with the blog in Activity 7.

9 Work in groups. What three new things would you like your area to have? Why?

10 **WRITING SKILL**   Using persuasive language

Choose one of your ideas from Activity 9 and write a blog post about it. Use the structure from the Writing strategy box.

11 Exchange blog posts with a partner. Check each other's work. Does it use the ideas from the Writing strategy box? Does it persuade you about their ideas?

Writing strategy

Persuading people to make a change

- Introduce your topic with a personal story.
- Mention successful examples of the change you're arguing for.
- Ask readers to think of their own experience and describe the emotional side of your proposal.
- Explain what's wrong and what would be right.
- End with a call to action that explains exactly what you think people should do.

We should have an art gallery. If we had one, then…

9 All in a Day's Work

Two women make fish nets at the fishing village of Vinh Hy, Vietnam.

9A Work should be fun!

VOCABULARY Jobs

1 MY PERSPECTIVE

Answer the questions.

1 Look at the photo. Would you like to have this job? Why?

2 Rank the aspects of a job from 1 (most important) to 5 (least important).

_____ Making a lot of money   _____ Working close to home
_____ Doing something you enjoy   _____ Doing something important
_____ Being part of a team   with your life

3 Do you agree with the title of the lesson? Why?

2 Match the jobs with the correct description. Use your dictionary if necessary.

1 _____ software engineer   **a** designs devices like smartphones
2 _____ electrical engineer   **b** gives people legal advice
3 _____ nurse   **c** helps people who are sick, usually
4 _____ doctor   with less training than a doctor
5 _____ accountant   **d** designs computer programs
6 _____ high school teacher   **e** helps teenagers learn
7 _____ chef   **f** prepares and inspects financial
8 _____ architect   information and money
9 _____ dentist   **g** designs buildings
10 _____ lawyer   **h** provides care for people's teeth
                                          i prepares and cooks food as a job
                                          j helps people who are sick, usually
                                               with more training than a nurse

3 Rank the jobs from Activity 2 from most to least needed. Each dot stands for one country that needs workers for the job. Check your answers on page 154.

1 _____ ·······················   6 _____ ········
2 _____ ··················   7 _____ ········
3 _____ ················   8 _____ ·······
4 _____ ···············   9 _____ ······
5 _____ ···········   10 _____ ····

4 Look at these jobs. Which category does each one belong to? Think of one more job for each category. Use your dictionary if necessary.

chief executive	cleaner	construction worker	factory worker
firefighter	manager	office worker	paramedic
police officer	salesperson	store manager	

1 Emergency services jobs   3 Trades
2 Office or desk jobs   4 Retail jobs

5 Work in pairs. Answer the questions. Use the phrases below.

1 Which of the jobs in Activities 2 and 4 would you most and least like to do? Why?
2 Are there other jobs not mentioned that you're interested in? What are they?

I'd like to be a(n)… because it's a(n) *interesting / exciting / fun / well-paid* job.
I wouldn't like to be a(n)… because it's a *dangerous / boring / difficult / low-paid* job.

LISTENING

6 Listen to Tomas and Julia talking about photographer Anand Varma. What's important to Julia in a job? What's important to Tomas? 🎧 54

adventure	fun	money	safety	staying near family

7 Listen again. Are the sentences *true* or *false*, or is the information not given? 🎧 54

   1 Julia would like to travel for work.
   2 Tomas has traveled a lot.
   3 Julia hasn't decided exactly what job she wants yet.
   4 Tomas says if you want to have a job like Anand Varma, you can do it.
   5 Tomas would like to have a job like Anand Varma's.
   6 Tomas says he'd like to be a doctor.
   7 For Julia, it's important to have an interesting job.
   8 Julia thinks Tomas should consider being a paramedic.
   9 Julia wants to make a lot of money.
  10 Tomas wants a job that's very exciting.

8 MY PERSPECTIVE

Think of a job you liked in Activity 5. What qualities or skills would you need for that job? Choose from the list below or think of your own ideas.

be brave	be a hard worker	be organized
be strong	good at cooking	good communication

Anand Varma is a science photographer and National Geographic explorer. In this photograph, he's at work in California, in the US.

GRAMMAR Past perfect

Past perfect

a *By the time he was a teenager, he***'d decided** *he wanted to be a marine biologist.*

b *He***'d** *already **had** a job working in a fish store when he started college.*

c *He got a job as an assistant photographer, but he **hadn't worked** as a photographer.*

9 Read the sentences in the Grammar box. Choose the correct words to complete the information below.

1 According to **a**, Anand decided to become a marine biologist *before / when* he was a teenager.

2 According to **b**, Anand worked in a fish store *before / after* he went to college.

3 According to **c**, Anand *had / didn't have* experience working as a photographer before he became an assistant photographer.

10 Which two verb tenses are used in each sentence?

Check page 144 for more information and practice.

11 Look at the timeline of Jacques-Yves Cousteau's life. Then use the words and time expressions to make sentences with the simple past and past perfect.

1 be 21 / discover love of the ocean (by the time)

_____

2 Cousteau / be in the navy for two years / travel around the world (when)

_____

3 Cousteau give 20 years of his life to the ocean / receive money from the National Geographic Society for his work (when)

_____

4 Cousteau write the book / *The Silent World* / make the film (before)

_____

5 Cousteau be a TV star / for more than 15 years / he receive the Medal of Freedom (before)

_____

6 he die / share his love of the ocean / with millions of people around the world (by the time)

_____

12 Make a timeline of your life. Include at least five experiences or things you have learned—when you began studying English, when you started playing a sport or musical instrument, when you discovered something you love, and so on.

13 Work in pairs. Make sentences with the simple past and past perfect to describe each other's timelines.

> *By the time you were eight years old, you had discovered that you loved art.*

> *When you were three, you had already started playing soccer.*

14 Work in pairs. With your partner, discuss one or two jobs that would fit each other's life experiences and interests.

> *You've played soccer since you were three. Maybe you could be a professional soccer player or a coach.*

TIMELINE OF JACQUES-YVES COUSTEAU'S LIFE

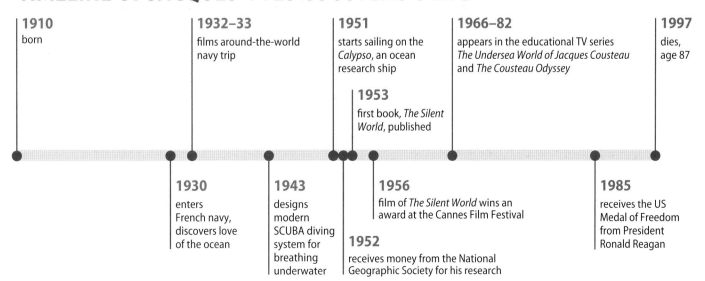

1910
born

1930
enters French navy, discovers love of the ocean

1932–33
films around-the-world navy trip

1943
designs modern SCUBA diving system for breathing underwater

1951
starts sailing on the *Calypso*, an ocean research ship

1952
receives money from the National Geographic Society for his research

1953
first book, *The Silent World*, published

1956
film of *The Silent World* wins an award at the Cannes Film Festival

1966–82
appears in the educational TV series *The Undersea World of Jacques Cousteau* and *The Cousteau Odyssey*

1985
receives the US Medal of Freedom from President Ronald Reagan

1997
dies, age 87

9B What do you want to be when you grow up?

VOCABULARY BUILDING

Dependent prepositions

Certain verbs are usually followed by a particular preposition. These dependent prepositions are followed by a noun or pronoun.

We **asked for** help.

Sometimes an object can go between the verb and preposition.

I **borrowed** a pen **from** him.

1 Read the Vocabulary Building box. Complete the sentences with the correct dependent preposition.

about	for	from	on	on	to	with	with

1 He applied _____ a job in a bank.
2 I agree _____ the idea of leaving school early if you want to start working.
3 They graduated _____ high school last year and found work immediately.
4 How much money you earn depends _____ how many hours you work.
5 Elementary school provided me _____ a lot of practice developing my social skills.
6 She introduced me _____ her brother.
7 You don't have to decide _____ a career in high school, or even in college.
8 Did you forget _____ our appointment?

READING

2 MY PERSPECTIVE

Do you agree or disagree with this statement? Why?

The main reason for going to school is to get a job.

3 Read the Tip. Then read the title of the survey. What are the three possible answers to the question in the title?

> Texts sometimes contain different points of view on a single topic. Understanding the different points of view can help you form your own opinion about the topic.

4 Read the title of the survey. Which two writers…

1 answer *No*? 2 answer *Yes*? 3 answer *Maybe*?

5 Read the survey again. Choose the correct options.

1 Lydia says that most of her school subjects were *useful / useless* for her job.

2 Sophia thinks school developed her *mind / study skills*.
3 Daniela learned skills for her job *at / after she left* school.
4 Paul believes that school sports develop *job skills / the body, but not the mind*.
5 Danh says that you study a lot of subjects to *prepare you for any possible career / discover what's interesting*.
6 Aslan says that paramedics and firefighters *don't learn their jobs at / don't usually finish* school.

6 Read the sentences. Who said each one?

1 History helped me develop critical thinking skills.
2 History is interesting, but not useful for my job.
3 The most important thing you learn about in school is yourself.
4 I don't remember what I learned in school.
5 School teaches you basic skills before you learn special skills for your job.

CRITICAL THINKING Identifying tone

> A writer's style of writing may affect how you feel about the subject. A pleasant or "warm" tone can make you like the writer. A negative or "cold" tone may make you want to disagree with them. A factual tone may consider more than one point of view and convince you to agree with the writer.

7 Read the Critical Thinking box. Then answer the questions.

1 Which of the writers has a negative tone? How can you tell?
2 Which of the writers has the warmest tone? Why?
3 Which two writers have a factual tone? How do you know?
4 Which answer do you agree with the most?

8 Read the responses below. Whose "No" answer is each one addressing?

1 I can see what you're saying. But the jobs you mention involve a lot of skills, not just one. In those jobs—and in your job—you need to be able to look carefully at situations and to solve problems, sometimes very quickly. Those are skills you practice in school.
2 I see what you mean. You learn facts at school, but that isn't the main reason for going. When you do schoolwork, you develop study and research skills, and you also learn to work with people in an organization.

9 MY PERSPECTIVE

Work in groups. Discuss the questions.

1 Think about the things you do at school. How do you think they prepare you for working life?
2 Which school subjects do you think will be the most and least important for your future work?

Workers putting together a car in Modena, Italy.

Does school prepare you for the world of work?

🎧 55 **An online survey* asked working people around the world if school had prepared them for their jobs. Here's what six of those people said.**

If you want to be a software designer and build an app,
5 you don't need to know about history, literature, or biology. When I applied for my first job, I hadn't learned any computer programming or project management skills. Learning facts about Ancient Rome and Ancient China was interesting, but I haven't used them in my
10 job. **—Lydia, software engineer**

My grandmother once told me that at school she hadn't learned what to think; she'd learned *how* to think. I agree with her. When we study history, we learn about people, politics, mistakes in the past, and the
15 history of great ideas. All of these things help us to understand our place in the world and to learn to think clearly. By the time I graduated from high school, I had definitely learned to think. My grandmother was right! **—Sophia, lawyer**

20 It depends on the type of job you want. If you want to be a teacher, then school is the perfect preparation. If you want to be a chef, school is a great start, but then you need something more—you need to learn all about

food. When I got my first job, my boss said it was the
25 beginning of my education. **—Daniela, chef**

When you play soccer at school, you learn about the sport—the rules, how to move the ball, etc.—but you also learn about working with a team. In most jobs, you work with some kind of team. Playing
30 sports at school definitely gave me a lot of teamwork skills. **—Paul, manager**

Most people don't become biologists, so studying biology may not be useful for your job, so in some cases, school doesn't prepare you very well. However,
35 school introduces you to a lot of ideas and subjects. You probably need to study biology to discover if you are interested in it or not. School helps you learn what you like and don't like, and then you can decide on the right career. Until my math teacher told me
40 I could become an accountant, I didn't know that job existed. **—Danh, accountant**

Not at all—or at least not for me. Does a paramedic learn to drive an ambulance at school? I don't think so. Does a firefighter learn to fight fires at school? Never.
45 Sadly, for most jobs, you don't need to know the things you learn in school. I forgot about school when I started working. **—Aslan, construction worker**

*Comments adapted from Debate.org.

Spanish racecar driver Carmen Jordá gets ready for another day at work.

"I entered my first go-kart race at the age of 12, but of course I was still going to school then, and I continued with my studies and university until I was 19. I started driving full-time at age 20."

9C She said it wasn't just about the money.

GRAMMAR Reported speech

① Look at the photo and quote. When does Carmen say she started racing? When does she say driving became her job?

② Look at the Grammar box with reported speech from the reading. Then answer the questions.

Direct speech	Reported speech
Sophia's grandmother: "At school, I didn't learn what to think; I learned *how* to think."	My grandmother once told me that at school she hadn't learned what to think; she'd learned *how* to think.
The boss: "This job is the beginning of your education."	When I got my first job, my boss said it was the beginning of my education.
The math teacher: "You can become an accountant."	My math teacher told me I could become an accountant.
Lydia: "I haven't used facts about Ancient Rome and Ancient China in my job."	Lydia said she hadn't used facts about Ancient Rome and Ancient China in her job.

1 How do the verbs and modal verbs change from direct speech to reported speech?
2 How do the pronouns *I* and *you* change?

Check page 144 for more information and practice.

③ Read Carmen Jorda's direct speech about her work. Complete the reported speech.

1 *My father took me to see my first Formula 1 Grand Prix at the age of eight.*
   Carmen said her father _____ her to see her first Formula 1 Grand Prix at the age of eight.
2 *At eleven I received my first go-kart.*
   She said she _____ her first go-kart when she was eleven.
3 *I've been working hard for a long time to get this opportunity.*
   She said she _____ working hard for a long time to get that opportunity.
4 *It has always been my dream. I train six days a week.*
   She said it _____ always been _____ dream and that she _____ six days a week.
5 *If one woman can do it, then many can achieve it!*
   She said if one woman _____ do it, then many _____ achieve it.

④ Complete the steps below.

1 Think about something that someone has said to you recently.
2 Write it down in direct speech as accurately as you can. Don't worry if you don't remember the exact words.

   This morning, my mother said, "You'll be late for school if you don't hurry!"

3 Write the reported speech.

   This morning, my mother said I would be late for school if I didn't hurry.

4 Work in groups. Share the reported speech you wrote down.

5 Listen to part of an interview with a teen soccer player who hopes to become a professional. Complete the interviewer's questions. 🎧 **56**

1 _____ becoming a professional soccer player?
2 _____ enjoy the most about soccer?
3 _____ played soccer?
4 _____ to soccer?
5 _____ to college?
6 Do you think _____ a scholarship*?

scholarship *money to pay for education for students who show special talent*

6 In your notebook, write Elena's answers to the questions from Activity 5 as reported speech. You don't need to remember her exact words.

The interviewer asked…

1 if she was thinking of becoming a professional soccer player.
2 what she enjoyed the most about soccer.
3 when she started playing soccer.
4 who introduced her to soccer.
5 if she would go to college
6 if she thought she could get a scholarship.

Elena said…

7 Work in pairs. Take turns asking the questions from Activity 5 and responding with your answers from Activity 6.

8 CHOOSE

Choose one of the following activities.

- Work in pairs. Write down five questions to ask each other about school or after-school activities. Ask and answer the questions. Then use reported speech to explain your partner's answers to another pair.

- Find an interview with an athlete or another celebrity that you admire. Write about what they said using reported speech.

- Ask some adults you know for advice about preparing for the world of work. Give a short presentation explaining their answers. Use reported speech.

Two high school students fight for the ball during a soccer game. For some students, sports are a way to get into college. Is there anything you think you could get a scholarship for?

The Surprising Thing I Learned Sailing Solo Around the World

> " When you're a child, anything and everything is possible. The challenge, so often, is hanging on to that as we grow up. "

DAME ELLEN MACARTHUR

Read about Dame Ellen MacArthur and get ready to watch her TED Talk. ▶ 9.0

AUTHENTIC LISTENING SKILLS

Weak forms

Often, words such as prepositions (*to*, *of*, *from*), auxiliary verbs (*are*, *was*), conjunctions (*and*, *but*), and articles (*a*, *the*) aren't stressed. These unstressed words are called weak forms. The vowel sound in a weak form is the schwa sound, /ə/.

1 Read the Authentic Listening Skills box. Listen to the sentences from the talk. Underline two weak forms in the first sentence and three weak forms in the second. 🎧 57

   1 When you're a child, anything and everything is possible.
   2 The challenge, so often, is hanging on to that as we grow up.

2 Work in pairs. Underline the words that could be weak forms. Then listen and check. 🎧 58

   1 I will never forget the excitement as we closed the coast.
   2 I will never forget the feeling of adventure as I climbed on board the boat and stared into her tiny cabin for the first time.

WATCH

3 Watch Part 1 of the talk. Choose the correct responses for each question. ▶ 9.1

   1 Which three of these did Ellen experience when she first went on a boat?
     a challenge   **c** excitement   **e** danger
     b adventure   **d** freedom   **f** relaxation

2 Which two of these things did Ellen do to reach her goal of becoming a sailor?
   a saved to buy a boat   **c** worked in a boat shop
   b read books about sailing   **d** took sailing classes

3 Ellen's school said that she wasn't smart enough to do what?
   a be a vet   **b** be a sailor   **c** go to college

4 When she was 21, Ellen met someone who helped her do which two things?
   a learn how to sail   **c** get a job in a company
   b design a boat   **d** sail around the world

4 Complete the experiences Ellen had when she sailed around the world. Then watch Part 2 of the talk and number them in the order she talks about them. ▶ 9.2

blown	broke	climbed	finished	hit	saw	took

   a _____   *Climbed* to the top of the mast (the highest part of the sailboat)
   b _____   _____ sunsets and wildlife
   c _____   Almost _____ an iceberg
   d _____   Were _____ over by the wind
   e _____   _____ everything she needed for three months
   f _____   _____ a speed record
   g _____   _____ in second position

5 Ellen says the race was both tough and amazing. Which experiences in Activity 4 do you think were mostly tough? Which were mostly amazing?

6 Watch Part 3 of the talk. Correct the sentences. ▷ 9.3

1 Ellen realized suddenly that the global economy is ~~different from~~ *the same as* living on a boat.
2 She decided to continue the job of sailing around the world.
3 She talked to chief executives, experts, scientists, and economists to teach them.
4 Her great-grandfather owned a coal mine.
5 According to the World Coal Association, there is enough coal for 180 more years.
6 Other valuable materials—copper, tin, zinc, silver—are not limited.

7 Watch Part 4 of the talk. Are these sentences *true*, *false*, or *not given*? ▷ 9.4

1 Ellen thinks we can stop waste in food packaging, car engines, electronic equipment, and food.
2 Ellen thinks we should use energy efficient light bulbs.
3 When Ellen's great-grandfather was born, there were 25 cars in the world.
4 Ellen says that computers are dangerous for the world.
5 Ellen says that her talk gives a plan for the future.
6 Ellen thinks young people should lead the change.

8 MY PERSPECTIVE

In the quote at the top of the page, Ellen says that anything is possible for children, and that the challenge is hanging on to that as we grow up. When you were very young, what did you think it would be like to be older? Is your perspective different now? How?

9 VOCABULARY IN CONTEXT

a Watch the clips from the talk. Choose the correct meaning of the words. ▷ 9.5

b Complete the sentences.
1 When I'm older, I'll have the *freedom* to _____ .
2 My *toughest* class is _____ .
3 If I go to college, I might *focus on* _____ .
4 I remember as a child feeling *curious* about _____ .
5 I had _____ but I *used* it/them *up*.

10 Work in pairs. Discuss the questions.

1 Ellen says her first trip was tough and amazing. What tough things have you done? What amazing things have you seen?
2 Ellen's dream job was to be a sailor. Think about your dream job. How could you use it to make the world a better place?
3 Have you had a moment when you "connected the dots" and started to think differently about something? What?

CHALLENGE

Listen to another extract from Ellen's talk. Answer the questions. 🎧 59

1 When Ellen learned more about the world's finite materials, what did she do?
2 What did she realize about the world's economy?
3 Ellen ends the talk by saying *Now we have a plan*. What is Ellen's plan?

9E What does a UX designer do?

SPEAKING Talking about careers

1 Look at the picture. Does this workplace look interesting or boring to you? Why?

2 Listen to part of a conversation between a student and a career counselor. Choose the best words to complete each sentence. 🎧 60

1 The student *enjoys / doesn't enjoy* using computers.
2 A UX designer helps make products that are *beautiful to look at / easy to use*.
3 A lot of UX designers work for *schools / banks*.
4 If you want to be a UX designer, you should study *art / science*.

3 Listen again. Complete the phrases in the Useful language box. 🎧 60

4 **PRONUNCIATION** Question intonation

Listen again to the questions from the conversation. Notice how the intonation rises or falls at the end of the question. 🎧 61

5 Work in pairs. Decide who is Student A and who is Student B. Turn to page 154. Take turns asking and answering questions about jobs.

Useful language

Talking about skills and interests

I _____ (computer games).
I get _____ in (IT). I _____ it.
I've always been _____ (software).
Art is one of my favorite _____ .

Asking about careers

What does (a UX designer) _____ ?
Where do (UX designers) _____ ?
What skills do (UX designers) _____ ?
Are (UX designers) well paid? / How much do (UX designers) earn?

WRITING A formal email

6 Read the email. Check (√) the information that the writer includes.

☐ the reason for writing
☐ information about the reader's company
☐ some information about the writer
☐ a question about how much Mr. Danoff earns
☐ questions about how to learn more about UX design
☐ a request for a reply

In many workplaces, people work together instead of having their own offices. Would you like to work like this?

Dear Mr. Danoff,

My school counselor, Ms. Wong, gave me your name and said that you could answer some of my questions about user experience design. Thank you very much for this opportunity. I'm in the tenth grade at the Quarry Hill International School. I'm very interested in both art and information technology, and I would like to learn more about being a user experience designer.

I have a few questions.
1. I want to choose some classes related to UX design. Could you tell me what the most useful subjects are? I'm planning to take classes in art, information technology, psychology, and design. Do you have other suggestions?
2. Do you know if I need a college degree to work in UX design? If so, could you recommend the best major?
3. I'd like to know if there's a website or magazine that would teach me about the business. I would like to learn as much as I can about what real UX designers do.

Many thanks again for agreeing to answer my questions. I look forward to hearing from you.

Yours sincerely,

Ignacio Suarez

7 WRITING SKILL Indirect questions

Read the Writing strategy box. Then read the email again. Underline how Ignacio asks the questions below in the email. Does he use direct or indirect questions?

1 What are the most useful classes?
2 Do I need a college degree to work in UX design?
3 Is there a website or magazine?

Writing strategy

Indirect questions are more polite than direct questions.

Direct question: *What do you like about your job?*

Indirect question: *Could you tell me what you like about your job?*

8 Choose a job from Activity 5. Write three direct questions about the job.

9 Now rewrite the direct questions from Activity 8 as indirect questions.

1 Could you tell me _____ ?
2 Do you know if _____ ?
3 I'd like to know if _____ .

10 Write an email to introduce yourself and ask for information about the job. Use the email in Activity 6 as a model.

11 Exchange emails with a partner. Check each other's work. Does it include the necessary information and use indirect questions?

10 Remote Control

IN THIS UNIT, YOU...

- learn about how technology helps us explore the world around us—and ourselves.

- hear about the history of communication technology.

- read about how artificial intelligence is changing how we think about technology.

- watch a TED Talk about how to control someone else's arm with your brain.

- express and support opinions.

Robots are starting to do many jobs people do. Do you think that is good or bad?

10A Inventions: Past, Present, Future

VOCABULARY Technology

1 Work in pairs. Answer the questions.

1 Look at the photo. What things do you see? Do you see any technologies that you know? What else do you think a robot like this could do?
2 Do you think this could really happen?

2 Throughout history, technology has changed how people understand and connect with the world. Read the facts about technology. Match the words in bold with the best category.

- When we think of (1) **technology**, we usually picture modern (2) **inventions** like smartphones, laptops, and tablets. But technology is anything we make or use that helps us do something or (3) **control** the world we live in. Even simple office (4) **equipment** like pens, pencils, and erasers were once important new (5) **developments**.
- Scientists used to believe that only humans made and used (6) **tools**, but in the 1960s, researcher Jane Goodall watched chimps go through a careful (7) **process** of taking leaves off small branches so they could use the branches to catch insects.
- (8) **Research** shows that nowadays, many people feel that (9) **progress** in technology is too fast. They say we need to think more carefully about the possible drawbacks.

a Four nouns for things people use: ____*1,*____
b Two nouns that mean *change* or *improvement*: _____
c One noun that means *a series of actions or steps to do something*: _____
d One verb that means *to make someone or something do what you want*: _____
e One noun that means *a careful study of something*: _____

3 Complete these sentences using these words. Then discuss the question from item 1 with a partner.

control	developments	equipment	inventions	process
progress	research	technology	tools	

1 Do we simply use our _____ , or does it _____ us?
2 Recent _____ have made computer _____ smaller and smaller.
3 People rely more and more on new _____ . But is this really _____ ?
4 _____ has found that these things aren't just _____ that we use when we need them—many of us pay more attention to our smartphone than to the people around us.
5 Trying to teach yourself not to look at your phone so often can be a difficult _____ .

4 What technologies do you use? Rank the technologies from most useful (1) to least useful (6). Compare your list with a partner. Are there other technologies you use often?

_____ computer
_____ phone
_____ TV
_____ printer
_____ tablet
_____ camera

LISTENING

5 Answer the questions with a partner.

1 Do you use an electronic device every day? If so, what device?
2 What kinds of problems can using electronic devices cause?
3 How many different ways of communicating can you think of?
4 Which way of communicating do you use most often? Why?

6 Look at the timeline about the history of communication technology at the bottom of the page. Match each type of communication below with a date on the timeline.

telephone

cell phone

next big thing

smoke

bird

smartphone

text message

7 Listen to the lecture and check your answers. 🎧 62

8 Listen again. Answer the questions. 🎧 62

1 What message was often sent by smoke signal? _____
2 Who used birds for communication? _____
3 Who probably had the first mail service? _____
4 Where did scientists develop the telegraph? _____
5 What was the message of the first phone call? _____
6 Why wasn't the cell phone useful until 1979? _____
7 When did email become popular? _____
8 What was the first text message? _____
9 What does the speaker compare new technology to? _____

9 Work in pairs. Discuss this question: What do *you* think could be the next big thing in communication technology?

The Pony Express mail service in the United States linked the East and West Coasts of the country.

Important dates in the history of communication technology

10,000 YEARS AGO	2,000 YEARS AGO	0–100	1400s	1830s	1876
1 _____	2 _____	Mail service	Mail service in Europe grows	The first efficient telegraph lines	3 _____

GRAMMAR Passive voice

10 Look at the sentences from the lecture. Underline the verb in each sentence. Circle the object of the verb.

1 The first smoke message was sent about ten thousand years ago.
2 The first telephone, as we know it today, was made in 1876.
3 The first text message was sent in 1992.

11 Look at the Grammar box. Answer the questions.

Passive voice

Active sentences talk about what a subject does:

Alexander Graham Bell made the first phone call in 1876.

Passive sentences focus on the action or the object of the action:

The first phone call was made in 1876.

1 The *first / second* sentence above says who did the action.
2 We make the passive with the verb *be + base form / the past participle*.

Check page 146 for more information and practice.

12 Complete the article with the passive voice of the verbs. Use the simple present or simple past.

Messages from space?
The RATAN-600 radio telescope in Russia (1) _____ (turn on) in 1974. It (2) _____ (build) to receive radio signals from space. Most of the signals are just "space noise," but sometimes scientists hear radio signals with certain patterns that they think may be messages. In August of 2016, a signal (3) _____ (receive) that was very different from the usual noise. When the signal (4) _____ (share) with experts around the world, they agreed that it was very interesting. Was it a message that (5) _____ (send) from another planet—a smoke signal saying *We are here*? No one knows for sure. Every possible message (6) _____ (study) carefully, and the work continues.

13 PRONUNCIATION Passive voice stress

a Listen to the sentences. Underline the passive verb phrases. Which part of the verb phrase is stressed: *be*, the past participle, or both? 🎧 **63**

1 An earlier message was received in the US in 1974.
2 The signal wasn't produced on Earth. It came from space.
3 Messages are sent from Earth into space every day.
4 Every time a cell phone call is made, or a TV or radio show is broadcast, a signal is sent into space.
5 Maybe this information is studied on another planet.

b Complete the rule.

Usually, *be* and the past participle have equal stress, or _____ is slightly stressed.

c Practice saying the sentences in Activity 13 with a partner.

14 Look at these examples of technology. Write a paragraph about one of the technologies and the ways that it is used. Use the passive voice.

_____

a pen	a smartphone	a computer

A smartphone is used in many different ways. First,…

15 Work in small groups. Read your paragraph. Think of other ways to use the technologies your group wrote about.

A pen can be used to…

Text messages can be sent with…

Art can be created with…

1962	1973	1992	2007	The future
First email	4 _____	5 _____	6 _____	7 _____

10B Can tech teach us?

VOCABULARY BUILDING

Word forms

Verb	Noun (thing)	Person
develop	(1) _____	developer
improve	(2) _____	–
achieve	achievement	(3) _____
(4) _____	equipment	–
disappoint	(5) _____	–
entertain	entertainment	(6) _____

1 Complete the table with the other forms of the words. Use your dictionary if necessary.

2 Complete the article with words from Activity 1.

A short history of artificial intelligence

Computer experts and software (1) _____ first began trying to create artificial intelligence (AI) in the 1950s. Their earliest (2) _____ included teaching computers to play games and do math. They thought they could create a thinking computer within twenty years, but that turned out to be a (3) _____—the job was harder than expected. In the 1970s, work on AI slowed down, though computer games based on early research became a popular type of (4) _____ . But in the 1980s, as computer technology (5) _____ , AI research started up again. Now, companies are beginning to (6) _____ everyday technology like cars and smartphones with simple AI that can answer questions and follow spoken instructions. This means that many of us now have AI in our pocket. What will happen next?

READING

3 Read the tip. Separate the text below into chunks with slash marks (/).

> Meaning usually comes from the interaction of groups of words (chunks), not single words.
>
> When Fan Hui lost a game of Go / in October 2015, / history was made.
>   about a time   who   what   when   what happened

The game of Go / was invented in China more than 2,500 years ago and is one of the world's oldest—and most complicated—board games. It is played with black and white pieces called *stones* on a board with a pattern of lines.

4 Read the first paragraph of the article. Separate the chunks.

5 Read the article. Underline phrases or sentences in the article that support these ideas. Compare your answers with a partner.

1 The game between Fan Hui and AlphaGo was important.
2 Fan Hui respected AlphaGo as a player.
3 AlphaGo wasn't programmed like other computers.
4 AlphaGo learned to play Go in a way that is similar to the way a person learns.
5 AlphaGo taught Fan and Lee some new things about Go.

6 Read the article again. Choose the best option to complete each sentence.

1 AlphaGo won because it _____ .
   a copied moves made by humans
   b made a surprising move
   c didn't follow the rules

2 AlphaGo _____ .
   a was programmed to win
   b can make about three million different moves
   c learned to play by practicing

3 Fan and Lee _____ .
   a learned from AlphaGo and became better players
   b were very angry that AlphaGo won
   c regret playing against AlphaGo

CRITICAL THINKING Counterarguments

> Sometimes, when people give arguments for an idea, they don't consider arguments against the idea. Thinking about possible arguments against an idea can help us to understand it better.

7 Read the Critical Thinking box. Can you think of arguments against the ideas below?

1 AIs are beautiful because they can learn, "think," and "feel."
2 If AIs get smarter than humans, we can learn from them.
3 Developments in technology are a form of progress and always improve human life.

8 MY PERSPECTIVE

Think of something that you have to do that an AI could also do. How might the AI do it differently? Could you learn from this?

9 Work in pairs. Think of a problem in the world today and imagine three ways that an AI could help solve it. Make a poster explaining the technology that you imagine.

Lee Sedol (right) makes a move against AlphaGo.

Playing against computers THAT LEARN

🎧 **64** When Fan Hui lost a game of Go in October 2015, history was made: it was the first time a human Go champion was beaten by an artificial intelligence (AI)—a computer program that can think. And in March 2016, history was repeated when Lee Sedol—one of the world's top players—was defeated. As Fan watched AlphaGo make an important move against Lee, he thought: "That wasn't a human move." Then he said, "So beautiful, so beautiful."

Usually, game-playing electronic devices are programmed to predict the possible results of a move, but they don't learn new moves or improve. AlphaGo is different. When it was built, the AI was given three million human Go moves to analyze. Then it began playing. Through the process of sometimes losing and sometimes winning, the AI developed its own style of play, and learned to "think"—some people even say "feel"—like a real Go player.

Are Fan and Lee disappointed about AlphaGo's achievements? Is our technology becoming too smart? Perhaps surprisingly, the two Go champions see it as progress. After he was beaten by AlphaGo, Fan began to play the game in a different way, and he improved. He won more games against other humans. Lee, whose experience was similar, said, "I have improved already. It has given me new ideas." In this case, human and machine are working together for the development and improvement of both.

10C Using Tech to Take Control

GRAMMAR Passives with *by* + agent

1 Read the data and the text. Then answer the questions.

> **Kenya data**
> Portion of the population who have
> • a bank account: 40%
> • access to clean drinking water: 63%
> • a cell phone (adults): 82%

Mobile money: better than a bank

M-Pesa **was started** in 2007, in Kenya **by** Vodafone. The technology allows users to keep electronic money in their cell phones. This money can be used to pay bills and buy things, or to get cash—all without having a bank account. And now, the system **is used by** adults who don't have a bank account in Tanzania, Afghanistan, South Africa, India, Romania, and Albania.

1 Which is used by more people in Kenya: a bank account or a cell phone?
2 How is M-Pesa used by people without a bank account?
3 What does the word *by* show?

Passives with *by* + agent

In an active sentence, the agent (the person or thing that does the action) is usually the subject:

*The **customer** transfers the money.*

In a passive sentence, use *by* to say who the agent is:

*The money is transferred **by the customer**.*

Check page 146 for more information and practice.

2 Rewrite the news headlines as full sentences in the passive voice.

1 Emergency services rescue British climbers in Italian Alps
British climbers in the Italian Alps were rescued by emergency services.

2 "Robot suit" helps disabled people walk

3 Doctor uses iPad to save man's life

4 Laptop connects village in the Andes Mountains to outside world

5 Farmers use iPods to scare birds

The M-Pesa program is so successful that there are now local versions in other countries.

3 Match each headline in Activity 2 with an article below.

a _____ A Japanese company has invented a "robot suit." <u>Disabled people wear the device to help them walk</u>. Strong pieces of plastic support the wearer's legs, and small motors make them move.

b _____ Two men were caught by bad weather high in the Alps near the French border with Italy. One of the men hurt his shoulder, so they had to stop climbing. <u>They sent a text message to a friend back home</u>. The friend then contacted Italian emergency services.

c _____ A US man with heart problems became ill while cycling. He asked a passing man for help, not knowing the man was a doctor. The doctor used his iPad to get information about the man's medical history, and this <u>quick action saved the man's life</u>.

d _____ In Kenya, farmers' plants are often eaten by wild animals. <u>In the Kasigau region, some farmers recorded scary sounds to put on an iPod</u>. Electronic equipment senses when an animal is near and the iPod plays the sound, which makes the animals run away.

e _____ Children in the village of Arahuay, Peru, were given laptops by the government. <u>The kids use the computers for their studies and to communicate with the outside world</u>. The government hopes the free laptops will help to educate the children.

4 Look at the underlined sentences in Activity 3. Rewrite the sentences using the passive voice. How does the passive change the focus of the sentence?

a _____
_____

b _____
_____

c _____
_____

d _____
_____

e _____
_____

Young children in the village of Arahuay, Peru, use laptops in school to stay in touch with the outside world.

5 Read the sentences. Cross out the agent when it isn't necessary.

1 The museum is cleaned every night by cleaners.
2 Homework is handed in each Friday by the students.
3 I was helped a lot by my friend Elliot.
4 The book was published by a publisher last year.
5 He was taught how to dive by his uncle.
6 His car was stolen by someone.

6 CHOOSE

Choose one of the following activities.

- Write five sentences about your favorite piece of technology. Use the passive (with *by*, where possible).

- Work in pairs. Take turns thinking of a specific electronic device or other technology, tool, or piece of equipment—something you use. Use the passive (with *by*, where possible) to describe it while your partner guesses.

- In a small group, brainstorm an idea for a new invention. Say what it will do, who will use it, and what benefits it will have. Use the passive with *by* where possible.

GREG GAGE

Read about Greg Gage and get ready to watch his TED Talk. ▶ **10.0**

AUTHENTIC LISTENING SKILLS

Reduced forms

When some words combine with *to*, some sounds are lost in speech:

going to ⟶ gonna
want to ⟶ wanna
have to ⟶ hafta

1 Listen to parts of the TED Talk where Greg Gage talks fast. You will hear each section twice. Work in pairs. Try to write down what you hear. Check your answers below. 🎧 **65**

   1 I want to do some demonstrations. You guys want to see some?

   2 So now I'm going to move away, and we're going to plug it in to our human-to-human interface over here.

   3 So now I'm going to hook you up over here so that you get the… It's going to feel a little bit weird at first.

2 Read the extract. Underline the expressions with *to* that you think will be reduced. Listen and check your answers. 🎧 **66**

So I just need to hook you up. So I'm going to find your ulnar nerve, which is probably right around here. You don't know what you're signing up for when you come up. So now I'm going to move away, and we're going to plug it in to our human-to-human interface over here.

3 Discuss in pairs. What do you think it would feel like to be controlled by a machine?

WATCH

4 Watch Part 1 of the talk. Choose the correct words to complete the sentences. ▶ **10.1**

   1 Neuroscience *is / isn't* usually taught in schools.

   2 *Twenty / Fifty* percent of people have a neurological disorder at some time in their life.

   3 You have 80 billion *neurons / electrical messages* in your brain.

   4 When the woman squeezes her hand, we hear the sound of her *arm / brain*.

5 Watch Part 2 of the talk. Write *true* or *false*. Correct the false sentences. ▶ **10.2**

   1 The green lines on the iPad show the thoughts. _____

   2 The signal from the woman's brain travels through the electrodes to the man's brain. _____

   3 When the woman moves her arm the first time, the man feels nothing. _____

   4 When the woman moves her arm again, the man's arm doesn't move. _____

   5 When the woman's arm is moved by Greg, the man's arm moves. _____

6 **VOCABULARY IN CONTEXT**

   a Watch the clips from the talk. Choose the correct meaning of the words and phrases. ▶ **10.3**

   b Look at the quote. What do the words *free will* and *agent* mean?

c Complete the sentences with your own words. Then discuss with a partner.

1 The most *complex* thing I know about is

_____

2 My teacher sometimes asks for a *volunteer* to

_____

3 An activity I want to *try out* is

_____

CRITICAL THINKING Analyze how a message is delivered

Speakers can deliver a message in many ways. These include: providing background information or facts, demonstrating an idea or technology, and comparing an idea or technology to another one. When watching a TED Talk, pay attention to how the message is being delivered. Think about why the speaker chose a certain method.

7 Greg thinks everyone should be able to use neuroscience technology. How does he deliver this message?

a He explains that a lot of schools have bought his equipment and that students enjoy using it.

b He gives detailed facts about how an iPad is able to show information about the brain.

c He says that his equipment is inexpensive and demonstrates that it's easy to use.

d He shows the audience that the man and woman aren't afraid of technology.

e He compares his equipment to more expensive technology and says his is better.

8 Read the questions. Take notes.

1 How could this technology be used for good? Think of three ways.

2 Could it also be used for reasons that aren't good?

3 If you could use the same equipment, what experiment would you like to try? What do you think the results would be?

4 Is it important for new developments in communication technology to be available to everybody? Why?

9 Work in pairs. Discuss your ideas from Activity 8. Try to think about how your partner delivers his or her message.

CHALLENGE

Greg's talk shows one of the possibilities of neuroscience, which is science about the brain and nerves. Can you think of other types of science you would like to learn more about in school? Is there technology you would like to have access to—for example, sound or video recording technology? Weather-science technology? Computer technology? Something else? How could the technology be used in class? Make notes about your idea.

In groups of four, discuss your ideas. Choose one type of technology you would like to have for your school. Then present your idea to the class. Give reasons why this technology would be helpful to learn about.

10E Who's in control?

SPEAKING Talking about pros and cons

1 Companies are making cars that can drive themselves. Would you want to ride in one of these cars? Why?

2 Listen to the conversation. What pros and cons of self-driving cars are mentioned? 🎧 67

3 What pros and cons of self-driving cars can you think of?

4 Listen again and check (√) the expressions you hear. Then, in small groups, take turns talking about the pros and cons of the things below. 🎧 67

- ☐ text messaging
- ☐ social media
- ☐ controlling someone else's arm with your brain
- ☐ artificial intelligence
- ☐ smartphones

5 Work in pairs. Discuss the questions.

1 Does communication technology improve communication or make people communicate less?
2 Does self-driving car technology make the world safer or more dangerous?
3 Is technology good or bad for the environment?

Useful language

Talking about pros and cons

Looking at two sides of an argument:

On the one hand…, but on the other hand…

Talking about pros

One good thing about (self-driving cars) is that…

(Self-driving cars) are good because…

Talking about cons

One bad thing about (self-driving cars) is that…

(Self-driving cars) can be a problem because…

Carmakers say self-driving cars are safer than traditional cars.

WRITING A formal letter of suggestion

6 Read the letter to the director of a recreation center. Answer the questions below.

Dear Ms. Smith,

I'm writing about the new "no-phones" rule in the cafe area. While I understand that loud telephone conversations are annoying, I don't think quietly sending and receiving texts or checking an app is a problem— especially if phones are put on silent mode. Also, I can see that using a phone while ordering or paying for food is rude to the staff, but when people are sitting alone at a table, texting doesn't bother anyone.

Can I suggest that you replace the "no-phones" rule with a set of "use technology politely" rules? For example:
- Think about the people around you.
- Put phones on silent.
- Don't use your phone when you're in the food line.
- Don't talk on your phone in the cafe area.
- No selfies!

These rules would stop the annoying behavior but would allow people who aren't bothering anyone to use their devices.

Thank you for considering this suggestion.

Yours sincerely,
Mika Thibeau

---

1 What rule is the writer of the letter unhappy about?
2 In what ways does the writer agree with the rule?
3 In what ways does the writer disagree with the rule?
4 What does the writer think should happen?

7 Read the rules. What are the pros and cons of each rule?

1 Students must not bring electronic devices to school. (Rule made by School Principal Sonja Sanchez)
2 No music is allowed on the beach or in the park. (Rule made by Mayor Rudy Patak)
3 Headphones cannot be worn in the recreation center. (Rule made by Director Julia Smith)

8 **WRITING SKILL** Making a suggestion

Now choose one of statements in Activity 7 and write a formal letter with a suggestion about it. Use the language from the Useful language box. Follow the structure of the model. Make sure to do the following:

- Say why you're writing and explain the difference of opinion.
- Make a suggestion.
- Support your argument.

9 Exchange papers with a partner. Check each other's work. Does it use the language and follow the model correctly?

Useful language

Making a suggestion

Explaining differences in opinion:
While I understand that… ,
  I think / don't think…
I can see that… , but…

Making a suggestion:
Can I suggest that…
It might be possible to…

Supporting your argument:
(These rules) would stop… , but
  would allow…

MODALS: OBLIGATION, PROHIBITION, PERMISSION, ADVICE

must, have to

Use *must* and *have to* + the base form of a verb to say that something is very important or is necessary—an obligation.

Must can be used when the speaker thinks something is important.
> You **must** remember to call David.

Have to is often used when someone else has made a decision or rule.
> I **have to** hand in my homework by 3:00.

Use *have to* to ask if something is necessary.
> Do I **have to** buy a ticket?

Questions with *must* are grammatical but can sound old-fashioned or formal.
> **Must** I buy a ticket?

must not and can't

Use *must not* + the base form to express prohibition or to say that it is very important <u>not</u> to do something.
> You **must not** enter this part of the building. (It isn't allowed.)
> You **must not** wear shoes in the temple. (It's very important that you don't wear shoes.)

Use *can't* + the base form to express prohibition.
> You **can't** park here. (It isn't allowed.)

Must not sounds stronger and more formal than *can't*. *Must not* can sometimes be shortened to *mustn't*, but this is not common in American English.

can and don't have to

Use *have to* to ask about what's necessary or allowed.
> Do I **have to** arrive at 8:00?

Use *don't have to* + the base form to show:

- that something isn't important or necessary.
> You **don't have to** wear shoes here. (But it's OK if you want to wear shoes.)

- that you can choose not to do something.
> You **don't have to** come to the meeting; it's optional.

Use *can* + the base form to give permission.
> You **can** use this computer to check your email. (It's allowed.)

Use *can* to ask for permission.
> **Can** I use my phone here? (Is it allowed?)

should and shouldn't

Use *should* and *shouldn't* + the base form to give advice.
> You **should** hire a private tour guide at the museum. You'll learn more that way.
> You **shouldn't** go on a group tour; it's too noisy.

Should is also used to ask for advice.
> **Should** I take my camera?

When *shouldn't* is used in a question, it implies that a speaker thinks the answer is already known.
> It looks like it's going to rain. **Shouldn't** you take an umbrella?

ZERO CONDITIONAL

The zero conditional is used to talk about facts and things that are generally true.
> **If / When** you practice, you improve.
> **If / When** you don't practice, you don't improve.

The zero conditional is formed using two simple present clauses. One clause uses *if* or *when*.

If / When clause	Main clause
If / When + simple present	simple present

Either clause can come first.
> You can't succeed **if / when** you don't try.
> **If / When** you don't try, you can't succeed.

When the *if / when* clause is at the start of the sentence, it is separated from the main clause with a comma.

We can use *if* + simple present as an imperative to give advice or instructions.
> If you see a painting by Banksy, take a picture of it.
> Don't forget to visit some art galleries when you go Buenos Aires.

1 Choose the best options to complete the sentences.

1 You *don't have to / can't* use your phone here. It's against the rules.
2 According to the rules, you *shouldn't / have to* say how old you are when you sign up for a social media account.
3 *Should / Can't* I wear a tie on Friday evening?
4 You *must / mustn't* return the library book.
5 We *mustn't / should* wear shoes here. We have to take them off.
6 *Have to / Can* I wear these boots to school?
7 You *can / shouldn't* wear that old T-shirt to school; it's too dirty.
8 We *don't have to / have to* dress up for the party; it's casual.

2 Put the words in the correct order to make sentences.

1 uniform / you / do / wear / a / to / have / ?
_____
2 arrive / must / we / for / on time / class / .
_____
3 can't / you / this / computer / use / .
_____
4 can't / midnight / after / they / phone / the / use / .
_____
5 to / this / for / have / pay / we / do / ?
_____
6 we / wait / shouldn't / Alex / for / ?
_____

3 Look at the signs. Complete the sentences with *must, can't, don't have to, can,* and *should*.

| 1 | 2 | 3 | 4 | 5 | 6 |

1 You _____ ride a bicycle on this road.
2 You _____ go exactly 50 kilometers per hour, but you mustn't drive faster.
3 You _____ eat or drink here.
4 You _____ watch out for children.
5 You _____ use your phone here.
6 You _____ stop.

4 Correct the mistake in each sentence.

1 You haven't to wear a tie.
2 I don't must forget my jacket.
3 You not have to pay; it's free.
4 They don't have to park there. It's illegal.
5 You should to change your shirt.

5 Match the two halves of the sentences.

1 Artists like it _____
2 It can hurt _____
3 You should ask permission _____
4 Artists sell their work _____
5 We learn a lot _____
6 Tourists look out for street art _____

a if people say they don't like one of your paintings.
b if they become well known.
c when people travel to see their work.
d when they visit big cities.
e when you want to paint in a public space.
f when we make mistakes.

6 Make zero conditional sentences using the information.

1 I have time / I paint
When _____ .
2 it can be beautiful / something is imperfect
If _____ .
3 we learn from them / we make mistakes
When _____ .
4 we practice / we develop our skills
If _____ .
5 you relax / you enjoy your work more
When _____ .

7 Use the words to write sentences with *you* + the simple present tense.

1 If / want / learn about painting / take a class.
_____
2 Try / see some street art / when / go to Paris.
_____
3 If / need / finish something / accept imperfection.
_____
4 Ask for help / aren't sure what to do.
_____

8 Complete the conversation with the verbs.

can find	get	go	google	know	try

A When you (1) _____ to Warsaw next month, (2) _____ to see some street art.
B Is there a lot of street art in Warsaw?
A If you (3) _____ where to look, you (4) _____ it.
B So where should I look?
A When you (5) _____ "Warsaw street art," you (6) _____ a list of art and artists.

PREDICTIONS AND ARRANGEMENTS

Predictions with *will*

Affirmative	Negative
I / You / He / She / It / They will eat.	I / You / He / She / It / They won't eat. (won't = will not)

Question	Short answer
Will I / you / he / she / it / they eat?	**Yes,** I / you / he / she / it / they **will.** **No,** I / you / he / she / it / they **won't.**

Use *will* + the base form of a verb for predictions that you are certain about.
> We **will need** more food.

Also use *will* + the base form for immediate decisions.
> *I'll go to the store.*

Negative sentences are formed with *won't* (*will not*) + the base form.
> We **won't have** a problem feeding everyone.

Questions are formed with *will* + subject + the base form.
> **Will** we **grow** food underwater?

Predictions with *might* and *may*

Use *might* / *may* + the base form to talk about possible future events or situations. *Might* is less certain than *will*.
> We **might discover** new sources of food.
> The population **may not increase** so quickly.

Future with *going to*

Use (*be*) *going to* + the base form to talk about plans or predictions.
> *I'm **going to be** in cooking school next year. It's **going to be** a lot of work.*

going to or *will*?

Going to is usually used when there is evidence for a prediction, especially when it is expected to happen soon.
> *I invited three friends for dinner, so we're **going to** need more food!*

Will is usually used for long-term predictions.
> *The world population **will** be about 10 billion in 2050.*
> *I'll get the phone.*

In many cases, there is no difference between *will* and *going to* for predictions.

> *Do you think 3D food printing **is going to be** popular?*
> *Do you think 3D food printing **will be** popular?*

Present continuous for future arrangements

The present continuous can be used to talk about plans for the future.
> *We're **meeting** after school today.*

In many cases, there is no difference between using the present continuous and *going to* when talking about future plans.
> *We're **going to give** our presentation next Monday.*
> *We're **giving** our presentation next Monday.*

When talking about future plans, a future time expression is usually used with the present continuous.
> *I'm **working** on my project <u>next week</u>.* (= future)
> *I'm **working** on my project.* (= now)

FIRST CONDITIONAL

The first conditional is used to talk about a possible or likely future. The *if* clause explains what must happen (the condition) for the future result in the main clause.
> **If** you go to China, you'll eat a lot of delicious food.

The *if* clause can be in two places:
> *You might meet some farmers **if** you visit the countryside.*
> ***If** you visit the countryside, you might meet some farmers.*

When the *if* clause is at the start of the sentence, it is separated from the main clause with a comma.

Forming the first conditional:

If + simple present, *will* / *won't* + infinitive (without *to*)
> *If we **don't allow** large signs on the street, businesses owners **will be** angry.*

may, might, could

May, *might*, and *could* can be used instead of *will* when possible events are less certain.
> *If you travel the world, you **may** discover foods you never knew about.*
> *You **might** eat fish for breakfast if you go to Japan.*
> *If you travel in Brazil, it **could** be difficult to find vegetarian food.*

When

For situations in the future, *when* is used to show that a speaker is sure something is going to happen.
> ***When** you go to Korea, you might eat bulgogi.* (You're definitely going to Korea.)
> *If you go to Korea, you might eat bulgogi.* (There's a possibility you're going to Korea, but I'm not sure you're going.)

1 Add *will* or *'ll* to each sentence.

1 Food _____ be more expensive.
2 We _____ eat less meat.
3 Robots _____ work on farms.
4 Some people _____ have food "printers" in their kitchen.
5 _____ people grow more vegetables at home?

2 Put the words in order to make predictions and questions.

1 may / We / more / grow / in / food / laboratories
_____ .
2 will / There / people / be / more / a lot
_____ .
3 there / Will / fish / enough / be
_____ ?
4 be / What / the / population / will
_____ ?
5 eat / They / fast / won't / food
_____ .

3 Complete the sentences with *going to*.

1 Look at the clouds. it *'s going to* rain on our picnic!
2 There's too much food. We _____ finish it.
3 There are two pizzas for thirty people. _____ we _____ have enough food for everyone?
4 This restaurant is very unpopular, so it _____ close.
5 The cost of raising animals is increasing. _____ meat _____ become more expensive?

4 Complete the sentences with *going to* and the verbs in parentheses.

1 _____ a vegetarian diet _____ (be) more popular in the future?
2 People _____ (eat) more plants that grow in the sea.
3 The typical home _____ (have) a big vegetable garden.
4 _____ restaurants _____ (serve) more local food?
5 I _____ (not change) my way of eating.

5 Match the situations below with the predictions or questions in Activity 4.

a _3_ People are becoming more interested in growing their own food.
b _____ When they eat out, people want to know where the food comes from.
c _____ A lot of people avoid meat these days.
d _____ I know what I like to eat.
e _____ The Japanese diet includes a lot of seaweed.

6 Write sentences using *will* or *going to*.

1 In the next 50 years / people live on Mars
_____ .
2 By the year 2100 / most of our food come from factories
_____ .
3 People like healthy food / so fast food be less popular
_____ .
4 Farming is difficult / fewer people become farmers
_____ .

7 Put *will* in the correct place in each sentence.

1 If we have enough farms, we *will* be able to feed everyone.
2 You have delicious honey if you visit Kars.
3 If they leave their villages, people forget their traditions.
4 If I make a salad, you stay and have dinner with us?
5 Hannah teach us some recipes if we ask her?

8 Choose the best word to complete each sentence.

1 If the bees don't transfer the pollen, fruit *will / won't* grow.
2 These plants don't like water, so they *might / might not* be healthy if you give it to them every day.
3 If we *don't meet / meet* any beekeepers, I'll buy some honey.
4 If we act now, we *may / may not* be able to save the bees.

9 Complete the sentences with the correct form of the words in parentheses. Use *will* and the verbs.

1 If you ___*choose*___ (choose) the restaurant, I *'ll make* _____ (make) the reservation.
2 We _____ (see) each other tomorrow if we _____ (not meet) tonight.
3 If they _____ (leave) home at 7:00, they _____ (arrive) at the restaurant at 7:30.
4 He _____ (bring) some food with him if you _____ (ask) him to.

10 Read the sentences. Write conditional sentences with the words in parentheses.

1 I want to try the new vegetarian restaurant. I might have time. (will / if)
I'll try the new vegetarian restaurant if I have time.
2 They want to buy some Turkish honey. They might find it in town. (may / if)
_____
3 The bees might be happy. Happy bees make a lot honey. (if / might)
_____
4 He will finish reading the book. He will know more about bees. (when / will)
_____

SECOND CONDITIONAL

The second conditional is used to talk about imaginary, unlikely, or impossible situations. The *if* clause explains what would cause the future result in the main clause.

> *If* I **had** more time for shopping, I**'d be** really happy.
> (= I don't have time for shopping.)
> *If* I **had** more money, I**'d buy** some new clothes.
> (= I don't have more money.)
> *If* I **were** taller, this shirt **would fit**.
> (= I am a certain height, and I can't change that.)

Forming the second conditional:

If + simple past, *would* + infinitive (without *to*)
> *If* I **were** you, I **would buy** the recycled cotton bag.

Notice that the main verb is in the simple past even though the sentence refers to the present or the future.

The *if* clause can appear in two places. When the *if* clause begins a sentence, separate it from the main clause with a comma.

> *If* you **had** a SellMyStuff account, you **could sell** some of your old things.
> You **could sell** some of your old things *if* you **had** a SellMyStuff account.

Would is generally used in the main clause, but to emphasize that something is a possibility, *could* or *might* can be used.

> *If* I **bought** this and didn't like it, I **could give** it to you.
> *If* it **weren't** too small, I **might buy** it.

The second conditional is different from the first conditional because the first conditional is used to talk about a possible or likely future rather than an imaginary, unlikely, or impossible one.

DEFINING RELATIVE CLAUSES

A defining relative clause gives information about the noun that comes directly before it and says exactly who or what the noun is. Defining relative clauses are formed with the relative pronouns *who*, *that*, and *which*.

> **The shop that** sells second-hand furniture is near here.
> **The person who** sold me this shirt made it.
> **Advertisements which** don't tell the truth are terrible.

The relative clause can define either the subject of the main clause (as in the examples above) or the object of the main clause.

> I know the **person who** made this shirt.
> I hate **advertisements that** don't tell the truth.

In all of the above sentences, the relative pronoun has to be included because in each case it is the subject of the relative clause.

> ~~This is the shop sells beautiful upcycled lamps.~~

If the relative pronoun is the object of the verb in the relative clause, the relative pronoun can be left out.

> These are the new shoes **that** I told you about.
> These are the new shoes I told you about.

Use:

- *who* to identify people.
  > The **guy who** runs the restaurant grows his own vegetables.

- *which* to identify things.
  > I couldn't find a **shop which** sold the kind of clothes I like to buy.

- *that* to identify people and things. Using it this way is less formal than *who* or *which*.
  > The **artist that** made this lamp lives in Madrid. The **work that** he does is really interesting.

Defining relative clauses can also be used to join two sentences together.

> This is a table. It used to be a traffic sign.
> This is a table **that** used to be a traffic sign.

1 Put *will* in the correct place in each sentence.

1 You see happy workers if you visit the factory.
2 If they design cool clothes, people buy them.
3 If I give you this shirt, you wear it?
4 David wear his new jacket if he comes to the party?

2 Put the words in the correct order to make sentences.

1 sell anything / we wouldn't / If we / advertise / didn't
2 your old clothes, / If you didn't / you could / throw away / recycle them
3 grow soy / They would / didn't grow corn / if they
4 would sell / The store / if it were / more / bigger
5 a coat, / you could / If / make it / I designed

3 Choose the correct options to complete the sentences.

1 If I have time on Saturday, I *would / will* go shopping.
2 We'd buy our clothes at a recycled clothes store if our town *had / has* one.
3 Will you *waited / wait* for me outside the store if I'm a few minutes late?
4 She wouldn't buy from this company if they *don't / didn't* pay their workers well.
5 If the billboards weren't here, this street *would look / looks* much better.

4 Complete the sentences with the simple present, simple past, and the *will* or *would* form of the verb.

1 If I buy the blue jacket, I ___won't buy___ (not buy) the red one.
2 Gregor will answer your questions if you _____ (have) any.
3 If you _____ (not care) about the workers, would you choose this shirt?
4 How would you feel if you _____ (work) in a dangerous clothing factory?
5 What _____ (you / do) if you can't find a shirt you like?
6 I _____ (not choose) that color if I were you.

5 Write conditional sentences using *if* and the words in bold.

1 He loves designing clothes. That's why he does it. **wouldn't**
He wouldn't design clothes if he didn't love it .
2 I don't have any money. I can't buy new clothes. **had**
_____
3 I don't know if you have any money. I can pay for these shoes. **don't**
_____ .
4 It may rain tomorrow. We may not go shopping. **won't**
_____

6 Choose the correct option.

1 I want to buy a jacket *who / that* isn't too expensive.
2 Is this the shop *which / who* sells old computers?
3 They're the guys *which / who* design the skateboards.
4 The person *which / that* made this chair also designs clothes.
5 Do you know a store *that / who* sells good used clothes?
6 My friend *which / who* runs his own shop lives in Rio.

7 Match the sentence halves.

1 The shop _____
2 I bought this shirt in a town _____
3 She's the person _____
4 Six is the time _____
5 He designed the clothes _____
6 They're the people _____

a which isn't far from Paris.
b that the shops close.
c who turn old clothes into handbags.
d that I wore last week.
e which I love is over there.
f who makes upcycled furniture.

8 Look at the table. Write sentences using relative pronouns.

Person or thing	What the person or thing is	Important information
1 Mr. Han	college teacher	teaches furniture design
2 Old to New	store	sells upcycled furniture
3 Di Garcia	designer	designed my shirt
4 China Square Central	shopping center in Singapore	has a weekend market for selling used things
5 The Sato family	our neighbors	own several clothing stores

1 *Mr. Han is a college teacher who teaches furniture design.*
2 _____
3 _____
4 _____
5 _____

PAST PERFECT

The past perfect is formed by *had* + the past participle.
She'd lived in Rio for ten years before she moved to Fortaleza.

The past perfect is used with the simple past to talk about completed actions that happened before a certain time in the past.

worked in Spain ⟶ worked in Peru ⟶ moved to the US
He'd worked in Spain and Peru before he moved to the US.

These time expressions can be used with the past perfect:
already, before, by the time, just, yet
They had already started class when she arrived.
He hadn't studied computer science before he went to college.
By the time she was twenty-two years old, she had written three books.
I'd just moved to Madrid when I met Marco.
When you got your job, had you finished college yet?

Affirmative	Negative
I / You / He / She / It / They **had arrived** on schedule.	I / You / He / She / It / They **hadn't arrived** on schedule.

Yes/No questions	Short answers
Had I / you / he / she / it / they **arrived** on schedule?	Yes, I / you / he / she / it / they **had**. No, I / you / he / she / it / they **hadn't**.

Past perfect and simple past

The past perfect is often used with the simple past to talk about the actions or situations that happened before a more recent action.
I had been on the boat for less than two hours when we saw our first whale.

REPORTED SPEECH

To say what another person said, use reported speech. In reported speech, the verb tense is moved backwards in time and pronouns, possessive adjectives, and adverbs of time and place are also changed. The most common reporting verb is *said*. Sometimes *that* is used after *said*.

Tense changes in statements

Actual words	Reported speech
simple present "You're a good writer."	⟶ simple past He said (that) I was a good writer.
present continuous "You're going to graduate."	⟶ past continuous They said I was going to graduate.
simple past "Her performance showed natural ability."	⟶ simple past / past perfect She said (that) her performance showed / had shown natural ability.
present perfect "You've worked very hard."	⟶ past perfect He said (that) I'd worked very hard.
will / won't "You'll be famous one day." "You won't forget your friends."	⟶ *would / wouldn't* She said (that) I would be famous one day. She said (that) I wouldn't forget my friends.
can / can't "I can help you." "I can't do your work for you."	⟶ *could* He said that he could help me. He said that he couldn't do my work for me.

said and *told*

An object is always used with *told*.

"I'm your new teacher."	⟶ He told us / me / them / you (that) he was our new teacher. ~~He told (that) he was our new teacher.~~

An object is never used with *said*.

"I'm your new teacher."	⟶ He said (that) he was our new teacher. ~~He said us / me / them / you (that) he was our new teacher.~~

In reported speech, the words that refer to people, times, and places need to be changed.

I ⟶ he / she / it / you
we ⟶ you / they
my ⟶ his / her / its / your
our ⟶ your / their
now ⟶ then
today ⟶ that day
tomorrow ⟶ the next day
yesterday ⟶ the day before / the previous day
last night ⟶ the night before / the previous night
here ⟶ there
this room ⟶ that room

1 Complete the article with the simple past or past perfect of the verbs in parentheses.

An early love for the ocean

Asha de Vos was born and grew up in Sri Lanka. As a baby, she loved the water and (1) _____ (learn) to swim by the time she was three. And by the age of six, she (2) _____ (decide) to become a marine biologist when she grew up.

A job on a potato farm

When she graduated from college in Scotland, Asha (3) _____ (take) a job working on a potato farm. Although she had tried during her final year of school, she (4) _____ (not be able) to find a job in marine biology, and now she (5) _____ (need) money because she (6) _____ (already decide) to travel to New Zealand to work on conservation projects—which she eventually (7) _____ (do).

Finding a career in marine biology

After she (8) _____ (work) for six months in New Zealand, she (9) _____ (get) a job on a research boat and traveled the world's oceans, looking at whales. Eventually, she (10) _____ (go) back to school and earned a PhD in marine biology. Now she's building a marine conservation research and education center in Sri Lanka to share her love of the ocean with others.

---

2 Look at the article in Activity 1. Write questions using the verbs in parentheses. Use the past perfect or simple past.

1 When _____ (you decide) to become a marine biologist?
2 _____ (you try) to find a biology job before you finished college?
3 When _____ (you realize) you were interested in whales?
4 How long _____ (you be) in New Zealand before you got the research job?
5 What did you do after _____ (you get) your PhD?

3 Look at the underlined verbs. Do they use the past perfect correctly? Correct the ones with mistakes.

1 When he called me, I <u>hadn't answered</u> the phone.
2 She talked to the career counselor and <u>had asked</u> for some advice.
3 They were expecting us because we <u>had emailed</u> and told them were coming.
4 I texted you this morning. <u>Had</u> you <u>gotten</u> it?
5 When I went to her office, she <u>had gone</u>, so we didn't talk.

4 Complete the reported speech.

1 "Your work is excellent."
  She said that _____ excellent.
2 "I learned a lot from your presentation."
  He told _____ he had learned a lot from my presentation.
3 "They've worked hard on their performance."
  She said that _____ on their performance.
4 "We'll be happy to help you."
  He told _____ to help me.
5 "I want to go to college."
  She said that _____ to college.

5 Write the direct speech.

1 He said he would see me next week.
  "_____"
2 She said she was interested in languages.
  "_____"
3 She said they'd started learning kung fu last year.
  "_____"
4 He said you practiced every day.
  "_____"
5 She said she would get a job to pay for college.
  "_____"

6 Read the conversation. Complete the reported speech below.

Davina I want to study art in college.
Ben Why do you want to do that?
Davina I really enjoyed my art class last semester.
Ben What did you like about it?
Davina It taught me to see. I've discovered a new side of myself!
Ben Will your parents let you study art?
Davina I'm not sure, but it can't hurt to ask them.

Davina said (1) _____ to study art in college. Ben asked why she wanted to do that. She said she (2) _____ her art class (3) _____ semester. Ben asked what she had liked about it. Davina said it (4) _____ her to see. She (5) _____ a new side of herself. Ben asked if her parents would let her study art. Davina said that it (6) _____ to ask them.

THE PASSIVE VOICE

Use the passive voice when the person who does the action is not important or is unknown.

Active: *Scientists develop new technology every day.*

Passive: *New technology **is developed** every day.*

The passive voice focuses the attention on the object of the verb: *new technology.*

Simple present passive

The simple present passive is formed with the simple present form of *be* + the past participle of the verb. Use the simple present passive for:

- facts that are generally true.
  *A lot of electronic devices **are made** in China.*
- regular actions.
  *Diving classes **are held** every Saturday.*
- steps in a process.
  *The devices **are designed** in California. After they**'re built** in China, they**'re shipped** all over the world.*

Affirmatives and negatives

The equipment	is / isn't	*made* in China.
Smoke signals	are / aren't	*used* today.

Questions

Is	the equipment	*made* in China?
Are	smoke signals	*used* today?

Simple past passive

The simple past passive is formed with the simple past form of *be* + the past participle of the verb.

Use the simple past passive for:

- facts from history.
  *The pyramids **were built** 5,000 years ago.*
- past processes or events.
  *After the battle, the town **was left** empty.*

Affirmatives and negatives

The area	was / wasn't	*explored* last year.
The caves	were / weren't	*discovered* in 1850.

Questions

Was	the area	*explored* last year?
Were	the caves	*discovered* in 1850?

PASSIVE WITH *BY*

To say who or what does or did the action (the agent) in a sentence in the passive voice, use *by.*

*New technology **is developed by scientists** every day.*

However, *by* is not usually used when the agent is:

- obvious.
  The first Apple iPhone was sold in 2007 (~~by Apple~~).
- unknown.
  My iPhone was stolen. (I don't know who stole it.)

❶ Choose the correct option (passive or active).

1 Technology *is used* / *used* for exploring the world.
2 Explorers *were made* / *made* the first map of the area last year.
3 I *was given* / *gave* this book last year.
4 *Were you used* / *Did you use* a computer at school?
5 The cave *was discovered* / *discovered* in 2007.
6 He *was found by* / *found* an ancient city in the desert.

❷ Complete the article using the correct forms of the verbs.

Genghis Khan (1162–1227) was the most powerful leader in the history of the world, but no one knows exactly where he (1) _____ (bury) when he died. The facts of his death (2) _____ (not know) today either. But explorer Albert Yu-Min Lin (3) _____ (hope) to find out more. In the past, people looking for ancient sites (4) _____ (explore) on foot and often dug a lot of holes. But now, small flying machines with cameras called drones (5) _____ (use) to take pictures from high in the air. These images (6) _____ (study) for signs of ancient buildings. If Lin's team notices something, they (7) _____ (not start) digging right away. A technology called ground-penetrating radar (8) _____ (use) to "see" what's underground without digging.

❸ Read the article. For each sentence, write *P* (passive) or *A* (active) and then choose the best word to complete the description.

Using technology to explore the world
Every day, new places (1) **are explored** thanks to some amazing technology. Cave diver Alberto Nava (2) **wears** a device called a "rebreather." When the diver breathes out, the rebreather (3) **cleans** the air before it (4) **is breathed** again. Rebreathers (5) **are used** when divers want to stay under water for long periods of time and when they want to be very quiet. A rebreather (6) **doesn't make** any bubbles.

1 _____ —the agent is *obvious* / *unknown or unimportant*
2 _____ —the focus of the sentence is on the *subject* / *object*
3 _____ —the *subject* / *object* is the focus of the sentence
4 _____ —the agent is *obvious* / *unknown or unimportant*
5 _____ —the agent is *obvious* / *unknown or unimportant*
6 _____ —the focus of the sentence is on the *subject* / *object*

❹ Write questions in the passive.

Simple present:
1 how / the air / switch on
    How is the air switched on ?
2 where / the equipment / store
    _____ ?
3 what / this machine / use for
    _____ ?

Simple past:
4 How many / maps / make
    _____ ?
5 When / this photo / take
    _____ ?
6 Which / cave / explore
    _____ ?

❺ Rewrite the paragraph. Put the verbs in bold in the passive and use *by* to show the agent.

Mobile health
In 2011, the Chinese government **started** the Wireless Heart Health project to help rural patients with heart problems. A small wire **connects** patients to a smartphone with equipment that records information about their heart. Then a doctor **checks** the information from the phone, any advice or a change of medicine can be given if necessary.

_____
_____
_____
_____

❻ Read the article. Answer the questions.

3D printing used by doctors to make tools and medical equipment
When Haiti **was hit by a huge earthquake** in 2010, the people needed medical equipment right away. However, sending things to Haiti is slow and **was made almost impossible by the earthquake**. Dara Dotz, who was working to help the people of Haiti, had an idea. A 3D printer **could be used by doctors** in Haiti to make some of the necessary tools and equipment.

1 What is the main focus of each sentence?
2 Which agent isn't necessary?

❼ Rewrite the bold passive sentences from Activity 6 as active sentences.

IRREGULAR VERBS

BASE FORM	SIMPLE PAST	PAST PARTICIPLE
be	was/were	been
become	became	become
begin	began	begun
bring	brought	brought
build	built	built
buy	bought	bought
choose	chose	chosen
come	came	come
cost	cost	cost
do	did	done
drink	drank	drunk
eat	ate	eaten
fall	fell	fallen
feel	felt	felt
find	found	found
fly	flew	flown
forget	forgot	forgotten
get	got	gotten
give	gave	given
go	went	gone
grow	grew	grown
have	had	had
hear	heard	heard
hurt	hurt	hurt
keep	kept	kept
know	knew	known

BASE FORM	SIMPLE PAST	PAST PARTICIPLE
leave	left	left
learn	learned / learnt	learned / learnt
let	let	let
make	made	made
meet	met	met
pay	paid	paid
put	put	put
read	read	read
run	ran	run
say	said	said
see	saw	seen
sell	sold	sold
send	sent	sent
sit	sat	sat
sleep	slept	slept
speak	spoke	spoken
spend	spent	spent
swim	swam	swum
take	took	taken
teach	taught	taught
tell	told	told
think	thought	thought
understand	understood	understood
wake	woke	woken
wear	wore	worn
write	wrote	written

UNIT 6 Explaining problems and solutions

Sometimes the title of the article will tell you what the problem is.

Look at the first paragraph. The problem and why it is a problem should be clearly stated.

The first paragraph should also say how the essay addresses the problem.

Look for each solution. Notice the supporting evidence the author uses. Using supporting evidence helps the author explain how the solution can help somebody.

Dealing with exam stress

It's natural to feel stressed when you have an exam. In fact, if you don't feel at least a little stressed, you probably aren't working hard enough. Stress can help make us study, but if we have too much stress, it can make us sick and reduce our chances of success. I asked my friends how they deal with exam stress. Here are their top six tips.

No one is perfect. Do your best but remember: It won't help you to have a lot of stress and worry about getting 100 percent every time.

When you're preparing for an exam, eat well. Your brain needs food! Eat plenty of fresh fruit and vegetables.

The concluding sentence should say what the author thinks will happen if you follow the advice. It might also restate the problem.

If you feel stressed out, talk to another student about it. It helps remind you that your feelings are normal.

You may want to stay up late studying, but you should get plenty of rest. If you're too tired, you won't learn as well, and you may get sick.

Exercise is one of the best ways to fight stress and clear your mind. When you're planning your exam preparation, you should include regular physical activity.

On exam day, remember to breathe. When you breathe deeply, you feel more relaxed!

If you follow these tips, you'll improve your chances of exam success. Good luck!

UNIT 7 A restaurant review

Make sure to answer these questions when describing a restaurant.

- Where is it located?
- What are the hours?
- What's the atmosphere like?
- What kind of food do they have?
- Is it expensive?
- What is the service like?
- Do you recommend it?

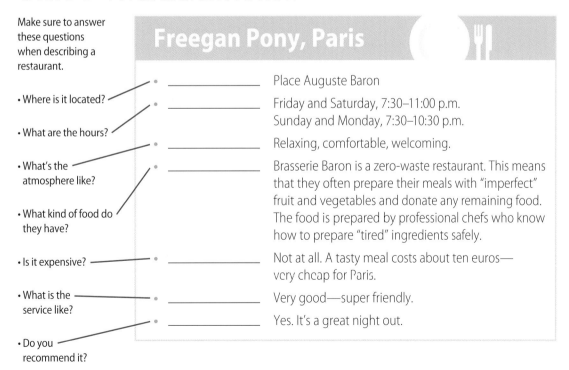

Freegan Pony, Paris

Place Auguste Baron

Friday and Saturday, 7:30–11:00 p.m.
Sunday and Monday, 7:30–10:30 p.m.

Relaxing, comfortable, welcoming.

Brasserie Baron is a zero-waste restaurant. This means that they often prepare their meals with "imperfect" fruit and vegetables and donate any remaining food. The food is prepared by professional chefs who know how to prepare "tired" ingredients safely.

Not at all. A tasty meal costs about ten euros— very cheap for Paris.

Very good—super friendly.

Yes. It's a great night out.

UNIT 8 A persuasive essay

State your opinion in the title or at the beginning of the essay.

Introduce your topic with a personal story. It can help people relate to your story. Include an example of what you're arguing for.

Clearly state what you want to change.

Mention successful examples of the change you're arguing for.

Explain how what you're arguing for could help people.

Ask readers to think of their own experience and describe the emotional side of your proposal.

Explain what's wrong and what would be right.

End with a call to action that explains exactly what you think people should do.

Making music shouldn't be a crime

When I went to Paris, I enjoyed the performers who played music, did tricks, or painted pictures on the sidewalk. My town doesn't allow street performers. We should change that.

The world's great cities have street performers: Tokyo, Edinburgh, Barcelona, Mexico City. If we allowed them here, people would come to watch them and would also shop. This would help the local economy.

How did you feel the last time you saw a great street performer? They make a connection with the audience, and they make visitors feel welcome.

Some people earn their living this way. It's wrong to stop people from doing honest work. It would be right to change the rules to allow street performers.

If we allowed them, it would improve our quality of life and give entertainers opportunities to perform. Please click on this link to join my campaign.

UNIT 9 A formal email

Include a polite greeting.

Include the reason for writing.

Say who you are. This can help you expand on why you're writing.

Say why you're writing. This can include asking questions.

Use indirect questions to be more polite.

Request a reply if necessary.

End with a polite and formal closing.

Dear Mr. Danoff,

My school counselor, Ms. Wong, gave me your name and said that you could answer some of my questions about user experience design. Thank you very much for this opportunity.

I'm in the tenth grade at the Quarry Hill International School. I'm very interested in both art and information technology, and I would like to learn more about being a user experience designer.

I have a few questions.
1. I want to choose some classes related to UX design. Could you tell me what the most useful subjects are? I'm planning to take classes in art, information technology, psychology, and design. Do you have other suggestions?
2. Do you know if I need a college degree to work in UX design? If so, could you recommend the best major?
3. I'd like to know if there's a website or magazine that would teach me about the business. I would like to learn as much as I can about what real UX designers do.

Many thanks again for agreeing to answer my questions. I look forward to hearing from you.

Yours sincerely,

Ignacio Suarez

UNIT 10 Suggesting a solution to a problem

Explain differences in opinion.

Make a suggestion.

Use specific examples and ideas of how your suggestion would work.

Support your argument.

Dear Ms. Smith,

I'm writing about the new "no-phones" rule in the cafe area. While I understand that loud telephone conversations are annoying, I don't think quietly sending and receiving texts or checking an app is a problem—especially if phones are put on silent mode. Also, I can see that using a phone while ordering or paying for food is rude to the staff, but when people are sitting alone at a table, texting doesn't bother anyone.

Can I suggest that you replace the "no-phones" rule with a set of "use technology politely" rules? For example:

- Think about the people around you.
- Put phones on silent.
- Don't use your phone when you're in the food line.
- Don't talk on your phone in the cafe area.
- No selfies!

These rules would stop the annoying behavior but would allow people who aren't bothering anyone to use their devices.

Thank you for considering this suggestion.

Yours sincerely,

Mika Thibeau

UNIT 9 Answers, Vocabulary Activity 3

1 software engineer
2 electrical engineer
3 nurse
4 doctor
5 accountant
6 high school teacher
7 chef
8 architect
9 dentist
10 lawyer

Source: Business Insider

UNIT 9 Speaking, Activity 5

Student A
Job: personal trainer
Duties: help people exercise and improve their fitness
Places of work: gym, health club
Necessary skills: good communication, organization, experience coaching
Personal qualities: lots of energy, high level of fitness
Pay: comfortable

Student B
Job: writer
Duties: write and sell books and articles
Places of work: office at home
Necessary skills: writing, good communication, ability to sell work
Personal qualities: able to work alone, able to finish work on time
Pay: very low to very high, depending on success

UNIT 6

able (adj)	/ˈeɪbəl/
accepting (v)	/əkˈsɛpt/
agree (v)	/əˈgri/
appear (v)	/əˈpɪr/
brave (adj)	/breɪv/
bravery (n)	/ˈbreɪvəri/
code (v)	/koʊd/
courageous (adj)	/kəˈreɪdʒəs/
(dis)advantage (n)	/ˌdɪsədˈvæntɪdʒ/
disagree (v)	/ˌdɪsəˈgri/
disappear (v)	/ˌdɪsəˈpɪr/
failed (v)	/feɪld/
impatient (adj)	/ɪmˈpeɪʃənt/
imperfection (adj)	/ˌɪmpərˈfɛkʃən/
imperfection (n)	/ˌɪmpərˈfɛkʃən/
impossible (adj)	/ɪmˈpɑsəbəl/
leverage (v)	/ˈlɛvərɪdʒ/
patient (adj)	/ˈpeɪʃənt/
perfect (adj)	/ˈpɜrfɛkt/
perfection (n)	/pərˈfɛkʃən/
perseverance (n)	/ˌpɜrsəˈvɪrəns/
possible (adj)	/ˈpɑsəbəl/
semicolon (n)	/ˈsɛmiˌkoʊlən/
socialization (n)	/ˌsoʊʃəlɪˈzeɪʃən/
socialize (v)	/ˈsoʊʃəlaɪz/
success (n)	/səkˈsəs/
support (v)	/səˈpɔrt/
supportive network (adj)-(n) (collocation)	/səˈpɔrtɪv/ /ˈnɛtwərk/
(to) code (v)	/tu/ /koʊd/
trial and error (phrase) (n)	/ˌtraɪəl/ /ænd/ /ˈɛrər/
unable (adj)	/ʌnˈeɪbəl/
(un)comfortable (adj)	/ˈkʌmfərtəbəl/
unsuccessful (adj)	/ˌʌnsəkˈsɛsfəl/

UNIT 7

achievement (n)	/əˈtʃivmənt/
appearance (n)	/əˈpɪrəns/
apple (n)	/ˈæpəl/
bear (v)	/bɛr/
bitter (adj)	/ˈbɪtər/
chicken (n)	/ˈtʃɪkɪn/
chili powder (n)	/ˈtʃɪliˌpaʊdər/
chocolate (n)	/ˈtʃɔklət/
coffee (n)	/ˈkɑfi/
cosmetic (adj)	/kɑzˈmɛtɪk/
corporations (n)	/ˌkɔrpəˈreɪʃən/
curry (n)	/ˈkʌri/
disappearance (n)	/ˌdɪsəˈpɪrəns/
discard (v)	/dɪˈskɑrd/

drink (n)	/drɪŋk/
farmer (n)	/ˈfɑrmər/
flavor (n)	/ˈfleɪvər/
food (n)	/fud/
french fry (n)	/ˌfrɛntʃ ˈfraɪ/
fruit (n)	/frut/
global (adj)	/ˈgloʊbəl/
guacamole (n)	/ˌgwækəˈmoʊli/
household (n)	/ˈhaʊshoʊld/
hunter (n)	/ˈhʌntər/
ice cream (n)	/ˈaɪs ˌkrim/
invested (v)	/ɪnˈvɛst/
kabob (n)	/kəˈbɑb/
lemon (n)	/ˈlɛmən/
lemonade (n)	/ˌlɛməˈneɪd/
organisms (n)	/ˈɔrgənɪzəmz/
pasta (n)	/ˈpɑstə/
pie (n)	/paɪ/
potato chip (n)	/pəˈteɪtoʊ ˌtʃɪp/
requirement (n)	/rɪˈkwaɪrmənt/
resources (n)	/ˈrisɔrsɪz/
salsa (n)	/ˈsɑlsə/
salty (adj)	/ˈsɑlti/
scandal (n)	/ˈskændəl/
shrimp (n)	/ʃrɪmp/
snack (n)	/snæk/
sour (adj)	/saʊr/
spice (n)	/spaɪs/
spicy (adj)	/ˈspaɪsi/
strawberry (n)	/ˈstrɔˌbɛri/
surpluses (n)	/ˈsɜrpləsɪz/
sweet (adj)	/swit/
tackle (v)	/ˈtækəl/
tea (n)	/ti/
tomato (n)	/təˈmeɪtoʊ/
traveler (n)	/ˈtrævələr/
type (n)	/taɪp/
vegetable (n)	/ˈvɛdʒtəbəl/
worker (n)	/ˈwɜrkər/

UNIT 8

advertises (v)	/ˈædvərtaɪzɪz/
air pollution (n)	/ɛr/ /pəˈluʃən/
ban (n)	/bæn/
be the change (phrase) (v)	/bi/ /ðə/ /tʃeɪndʒ/
campaign (n)	/kæmˈpeɪn/
design (v)	/dɪˈzaɪn/
do something about it (phrase) (v)	/du/ /ˈsʌmθɪŋ/ /əˈbaʊt/ /ɪt/
go for it (phrase) (v)	/goʊ/ /fɔr/ /ɪt/
governor (n)	/ˈgʌvərnər/
grows (v)	/groʊz/
hunger strike (n)	/ˈhʌŋgər ˌstraɪk/

inspired (v)	/ɪnˈspaɪrd/
make that difference (phrase) (v)	/meɪk/ /ðæt/ /ˈdɪfərəns/
manufacture (v)	/ˌmænjəˈfæktʃər/
material (n)	/məˈtɪriəl/
paradise (n)	/ˈpærədaɪs/
pick (v)	/pɪk/
produce (v)	/prəˈdus/
rainforests (n)	/ˈreɪnfɔrɪsts/
recycle (v)	/ˌriˈsaɪkəl/
recycling program (n)	/ˌriˈsaɪklɪŋ/ /ˈproʊgræm/
sealife (n)	/silaɪf/
sell (v)	/sɛl/
shopping bags (n)	/ˈʃɑpɪŋ ˌbæg/
throw away (phrase) (v)	/θroʊ/ /əˈweɪ/
walk your talk (phrase) (v)	/wɑk/ /jɔr/ /tɑk/

UNIT 9

accountant (n)	/əˈkaʊntənt/
agree with (phrase) (v)	/əˈgri/ /wɪð/
apply for (phrase) (v)	/əˈplaɪ/ /fɔr/
apprenticeship (n)	/əˈprɛntɪsʃɪp/
architect (n)	/ˈɑrkətɛkt/
be part of a team (phrase) (v)	/bi/ /pɑrt/ /ʌv/ /əɪ/ /tim/
broke the world record (phrase) (v)	/broʊk/ /ðə/ /wɜrld/ /rɛˈkərd/
chef (n)	/ʃɛf/
(chief) executive (n)	/tʃif/ /ɪgˈzɛk.jə.t̬ɪv/
construction worker (n)	/kənˈstrʌkʃən/ /ˈwɜ·kər/
curiosity (n)	/ˌkjʊriˈɑsəti/
decide on (phrase) (v)	/dɪˈsaɪd/ /ɑn/
dentist (n)	/ˈdɛntɪst/
do something useful (phrase) (v)	/du/ /ˈsʌmθɪŋ/ /ˈjusfəl/
do something you enjoy (phrase) (v)	/du/ /ˈsʌmθɪŋ/ /ju/ /ɪnˈdʒɔɪ/
doctor (n)	/ˈdɑktər/
economy (n)	/iˈkɑnəmi/
electrical engineer (n)	/iˌlɛkˈtrɪkəl/ /ˌɛndʒɪnɛr/
factory worker (n)	/ˈfæktəri/ /ˈwɜ·kər/
finite (adj)	/ˈfaɪnaɪt/
firefighter (n)	/ˈfaɪərˌfaɪtər/
focus on (v)	/ˈfoʊkəs/ /ɑn/
forget about (phrase) (v)	/fərˈgɛt/ /əˈbaʊt/
foundation (n)	/faʊnˈdeɪʃən/
freedom (n)	/ˈfridəm/
global (adj)	/ˈgloʊbəl/
graduate from (phrase) (v)	/ˈgrædʒuaɪt/ /frɑm/

high school teacher (n)	/ˈhaɪˌskul/ /ˈtitʃər/	tools (n)	/tulz/
interests (n)	/ˈɪntrɛsts/	try it out (v)	/traɪ/ /ɪt/ /aʊt/
introduce to (phrase) (v)	/ˌɪntrəˈdus/ /tu/	volunteer (n)	/ˌvɑlənˈtɪr/
lawyer (n)	/ˈlɔɪər/	weird (adj)	/wɪrd/
make money (phrase) (v)	/meɪk/ /ˈmʌni/		
manager (n)	/ˈmænədʒər/		
materials (n)	/məˈtriəlz/		
nurse (n)	/nɜrs/		
officer worker (n)	/ˈɔfɪs/ /ˈwɝkər/		
paramedic (n)	/ˌpærəˈmɛdɪk/		
police officer (n)	/pəˈlis ˌɑfɪsər/		
provide with (phrase) (v)	/prəˈvaɪd/ /wɪð/		
salesperson (n)	/ˈseɪlzˌpɜrsən/		
software engineer (n)	/ˈsɔftwɛr/ /ˌɛndʒɪnɪr/		
store manager (n)	/stɔr/ /ˈmænədʒər/		
tough (adj)	/tʌf/		
use up (phrase) (v)	/juz/ /ʌp/		
work close to home (phrase) (v)	/wɜrk/ /kloʊs /tu/ /hoʊm/		

UNIT 10

achieve (v)	/əˈtʃiv/
achievement (n)	/əˈtʃivmənt/
achiever (n)	/əˈtʃivər/
control (v)	/kənˈtroʊl/
develop (v)	/dɪˈvɛləp/
developer (n)	/dɪˈvɛləpər/
development (n)	/dɪˈvɛləpmənt/
disappoint (v)	/ˌdɪsəˈpɔɪnt/
disappointment (n)	/ˌdɪsəˈpɔɪntmənt/
discharge (v)	/dɪsˈtʃɑrdʒ/
electrodes (n)	/iˈlɛk.troʊdz/
entertain (v)	/ɛntərˈteɪn/
entertainer (n)	/ɛntərˈteɪnər/
entertainment (n)	/ɛntərˈteɪnmənt/
equip (v)	/ɪˈkwɪp/
equipment (n)	/ɪˈkwɪpmənt/
improve (v)	/ɪmˈpruv/
improvement (n)	/ɪmˈpruvmənt/
inventions (n)	/ɪnˈvɛnʃənz/
muscles (n)	/ˈmʌsəlz/
neurological disorder (n)	/nʊrəlɑdʒɪkəl/ /dɪsɔrdər/
neurons (n)	/ˈnʊrɑnz/
neuroscience (n)	/njʊrosajəns/
process (n)	/ˈprɑsɛs/
progress (n)	/ˈprɑgrɛs/
research (n)	/ˈrisərtʃ/
signals (n)	/ˈsɪgnəl/
spinal cord (n)	/ˌspaɪnəlˈkɔrd/
squeeze (v)	/skwiz/
technology (n)	/tɛkˈnɑlədʒi/

CREDITS

PERSPECTIVES

1

Workbook

NATIONAL
GEOGRAPHIC
LEARNING

Australia · Brazil · Mexico · Singapore · United Kingdom · United States

Perspectives 1

Publisher: Sherrise Roehr

Executive Editor: Sarah Kenney

Project Manager: Katherine Carroll

Media Researcher: Leila Hishmeh

Senior Technology Product Manager:
Lauren Krolick

Director of Global Marketing: Ian Martin

Product Marketing Manager:
Anders Bylund

Sr. Director, ELT & World Languages:
Michael Burggren

Production Manager: Daisy Sosa

Senior Print Buyer: Mary Beth Hennebury

Composition: Lumina Datamatics, Inc.

Cover/Text Design: Brenda Carmichael

Art Director: Brenda Carmichael

Cover Image: Bernardo Galmarini/
Alamy Stock Photo

For product information and technology assistance, contact us at
Cengage Learning Customer & Sales Support, cengage.com/contact

For permission to use material from this text or product,
submit all requests online at **cengage.com/permissions**
Further permissions questions can be emailed to
permissionrequest@cengage.com

Perspectives 1 Workbook

ISBN: 978-1-337-29731-8

National Geographic Learning
20 Channel Center Street
Boston, MA 02210
USA

National Geographic Learning, a Cengage Learning Company, has a mission to bring the world to the classroom and the classroom to life. With our English language programs, students learn about their world by experiencing it. Through our partnerships with National Geographic and TED Talks, they develop the language and skills they need to be successful global citizens and leaders.

Locate your local office at **international.cengage.com/region**

Visit National Geographic Learning online at **NGL.Cengage.com/ELT**
Visit our corporate website at **www.cengage.com**

Printed in China
Print Number: 01   Print Year: 2018

CONTENTS

6A The Best I Can Be

VOCABULARY

1 Review Choose the correct words to complete the sentences.

1 Riko enjoys meeting new people. She's very *worried / relaxed / friendly*.
2 The students are quiet because they are *nervous / relaxed / afraid* about the test.
3 Ana is *relaxed / afraid / shy* to fly.
4 They are *friendly / shy / worried* about money.
5 Alana was *nervous / relaxed / friendly* during her vacation. She enjoyed it.
6 Rafael doesn't talk in class because he's *relaxed / friendly / shy*.

2 Review Match the words to the definitions.

1 a place where there are a lot of office buildings _____
2 not quiet or boring _____
3 not old-fashioned _____
4 a place where there are a lot of houses or apartments _____
5 an area that people visit when they want to buy things _____
6 not too far; safe for people traveling on foot _____
7 full of people _____
8 from an important time in the past _____
9 not rural _____
10 in an area outside of a city _____
11 an old way of doing things _____

a urban
b walkable
c business district
d traditional
e modern
f historic
g suburban
h shopping district
i crowded
j residential area
k lively

3 Put the words into the correct categories.

accept	accepting	fail	failed
failure	imperfect	imperfection	perfect
perfection	reject	succeed	success
successful	unsuccessful		

Positive	Negative

4 Match the sentence halves to complete the definitions.

1 Something **perfect**
2 When something **fails**,
3 A **success**
4 Something that has **imperfections**
5 When you **accept** something,
6 A **failure**
7 When you **reject** something,

a is a bad result.
b is not perfect.
c it finishes without success.
d you think it's OK.
e you don't think it's OK.
f has a good result.
g has no mistakes or problems.

5 Put the words into the correct categories.

accept	fail	failure	imperfect
imperfection	perfect	perfection	reject
succeed	success	successful	unsuccessful

Noun	Verb	Adjective

6 Complete the sentences with the correct form of *be*, *have*, or *have to*.

1 You don't have to _____ perfect. Just try your best.
2 Don't buy that mirror. It _____ an imperfection on the glass.

3 The brothers opened a restaurant last year, but it _____ unsuccessful and it closed.

4 Jake, you _____ accept it. Your vision _____ imperfect. You need glasses!

5 She didn't get on the team. Now she thinks she _____ a failure.

6 This _____ perfect! I want to buy it.

7 She _____ a successful design business in the city.

7 Choose the correct word to complete each sentence.

1 The students work hard in order to _____.
a perfection   **b** success   **c** succeed

2 Sometimes it's hard to _____ failure.
a accept   **b** imperfect   **c** reject

3 The worst _____ is to not try.
a success   **b** failure   **c** imperfection

4 People have different ideas about what it means to be _____.
a succeed   **b** perfection   **c** successful

5 Young people often feel a need to be _____.
a imperfect   **b** perfect   **c** succeed

6 You can learn from _____, but you can also learn from failure.
a success   **b** successful   **c** perfect

7 Remember that nobody's _____.
a perfect   **b** imperfect   **c** accepting

8 People who always look for _____ will be unhappy.
a failure   **b** imperfection   **c** perfection

8 Listen. Write the correct word to complete each sentence. 🎧 **59**

accept	failure	imperfect	imperfections
perfect	reject	successful	

1 Teachers _____ that students will make mistakes as they learn English.

2 But some students are not accepting their own _____ English.

3 They think making mistakes means _____.

4 They don't want to speak until their English is _____.

5 These students need to _____ the fear of failure and start talking.

6 _____ students work hard and try to learn from their mistakes.

7 The best way to improve _____ is to practice.

9 Extension   Choose the correct word to complete each sentence.

1 She owns a very *successful / success / accepting* company.

2 My friend had a bad week. He *failed / rejected / succeeded* two exams.

3 Buy this fruit. It costs less because it has *perfect / imperfect / imperfections*.

4 This author's first book was very *successful / perfect / accepting*, and it made her famous.

5 An apple is a(n) *perfect / successful / accepted* example of a healthy snack.

6 Items such as clothing and furniture that are slightly *failed / imperfect / rejected* usually cost less.

7 I was locked out of my phone after three *unsuccessful / imperfect / accepted* attempts to unlock it with my code!

8 Studying in an English-speaking country is a(n) *perfect / successful / accepted* opportunity to improve your English.

10 Extension   Re-order the words to make sentences.

1 car / in / condition / is / father's / my / perfect
_____
_____

2 Miguel's / rejected / group / idea / the
_____
_____

3 skiing / winter / Minato / attempt / at / last / made / unsuccessful / an
_____
_____

4 more / success / is / or / academic / economic / important
_____
_____?

5 actions / accept / have to / responsibility / for / their / they
_____
_____

6 a / Kanna / example / a / of / student / hard-working / perfect / is
_____
_____

PRONUNCIATION

11 Listen and underline the reduced forms you hear. You will not underline words in all items. 🎧 **60**

1 Students have to show a student ID to enter the library.
2 Lucas doesn't want to work today but he has to.
3 No, you don't have to complete the assignment today.
4 I don't have to get up early but I do.
5 Turn off your phone now. Everyone has to.

LISTENING

12 Listen to the conversation. Answer the questions. 🎧 **61**

1 Why is the man going to the museum?
a for an assignment
b for fun
c for his art class
d for his job

2 What is the problem?
a He is busy on Saturday.
b He can't get to the museum.
c He doesn't like art museums.
d He isn't a good student.

3 What does the man have to do?
a choose a gift in the gift shop
b choose a painting or sculpture and draw it
c choose a museum to go to
d choose a painting and write about it

13 Listen and answer the questions. 🎧 **62**

1 Where would you hear this announcement?
a on the radio
b on television
c in school
d in a store

2 What is the purpose of the announcement?
a to provide information about closing time
b to give a weather update
c to report on road conditions
d to say that the wifi is not working

3 When will the store open again?
a after the snow stops
b after tomorrow
c before Thursday
d after 3pm tomorrow

14 Listen and answer the questions. 🎧 **63**

1 According to the fruit seller, the fruit is _____.
a perfect
b imperfect
c damaged

2 The fruit arrangement includes _____.
a orange
b banana
c apple

3 There are two kinds of _____.
a apple
b melon
c pear

4 The type of container chosen is a _____.
a box
b basket
c bowl

5 The customer wants a gift sent to _____.
a her home
b Chicago
c Macedonia

6 The bowl is _____.
a imperfect
b traditional
c perfect

7 The price includes _____.
a an additional bowl
b free delivery
c insurance

15 Listen to the conversations. Answer the questions. 🎧 **64**

1 How do the speakers describe the vegetables?
a perfect
b not perfect
c expensive

2 What is the student asking about?
a a class
b a text
c a test

3 What are the speakers talking about?
a weekend plans
b success stories
c travel

4 How was the woman's presentation?
a a failure
b perfect
c unsuccessful

GRAMMAR Modals: obligation, prohibition, permission, advice

16 Match the statements with the instructions or information.

1 You can't talk in this room.
2 You can't pay with a credit or debit card.
3 You must be a student to enter the library.
4 I have to finish my homework today.
5 I should go to a tutor for help with English.

a *Students must turn in their assignments tomorrow.*
b *Students only. Please show your ID.*
c *Quiet, please!*
d *Tutors available Tuesday and Thursday afternoons.*
e *Cash only.*

17 Read each sentence. Change the modal to rewrite it as a negative sentence.

1 At our school students have to wear a uniform.

_____

2 Students should use social media every day.

_____

3 Our coach says we must eat right before a game.

_____

4 You have to have a password to use the wifi.

_____

5 We have to be quiet.

_____

6 I can call you tonight.

_____

7 You should close your social media account.

_____

8 Students have to pay to use the pool.

_____

18 Complete the sentences. There may be more than one correct answer.

can	can't	don't have to	have to
must	should	shouldn't	

You (1) _____ follow these rules in yoga class. You (2) _____ wear shoes in the yoga studio. Leave your shoes outside. You (3) _____ use a yoga mat, but you (4) _____ bring your own. You (5) _____ use the mats the studio provides. You (6) _____ talk in the yoga class. You (7) _____ be quiet. You (8) _____ wear comfortable clothes. You (9) _____ try to do exercises that you're not ready for. You (10) _____ be patient. Yoga takes practice!

19 Complete the sentences with the correct modals.

1 It's going to rain. You _____ take an umbrella.
2 At this restaurant you _____ wear jeans.
3 Students _____ pay to visit the museum. It's free for students.
4 You _____ bring a small gift for your friend's parents.
5 Football players _____ wear any jewelry during the game.
6 People _____ turn off their phones in the movie theater.
7 Customers _____ use the cafe's wifi. It's free.
8 No, you _____ learn German. You should study English instead.

20 Choose the correct modals to complete the sentences. Choose all answers that are correct.

1 You _____ be 18 years old to have a driver's license.
   a must   b have to   c should
2 You _____ text Antonio and ask him to give you a ride to school.
   a couldn't   b should   c can't
3 Students _____ use their phones during the exam.
   a can't   b don't have to   c must not
4 She _____ read more books in English.
   a should   b can   c must not
5 In my opinion, restaurants _____ waste food.
   a shouldn't   b can't   c should
6 You _____ talk on the phone in the movie theater.
   a don't have to   b must not   c can't
7 When you don't understand something, you _____ ask a question.
   a should   b must not   c don't have to
8 You _____ take photos in the museum.
   a have to   b can   c must

6B Less Than Perfect

VOCABULARY BUILDING

1 The words and the prefixes form other words. Write each word in the correct category of the prefix that makes it form another word.

active	agree	connect	correct
direct	finished	honest	kind
like	lucky	mature	~~perfect~~
proper	successful		

dis	im	in	un
	perfect		

READING

2 Do the statements match the information in the article? Write true (T), false (F), or not given (NG).

1 The museum exhibit is unusual. ___
2 The exhibit includes perfect and imperfect items. ___
3 A coin that is not round might be something you could find on display in this museum. ___
4 All of the imperfect items are valuable. ___
5 The exhibit shows that *perfect* means the same thing to all cultures. ___
6 Artists had to reject items that were unusable. ___
7 The exhibit shows that all imperfections are mistakes. ___

3 Read the article. Choose the correct answers.

1 The meaning of the word *circular* in paragraph 2 is similar to
  a whole.
  b metal.
  c silver.
  d round.

2 In paragraph 2, why does the author include information that the imperfect items were found in many parts of the world?
  a To provide evidence that the items are from more than one culture.
  b To show that the exhibit is international.
  c To encourage people from all over the world to see the exhibit.
  d To explain why some items are glass and others are metal.

3 Which of the following can be inferred from paragraph 3?
  a *Perfect* and *imperfect* mean the same in all cultures.
  b The creators of the exhibit believe it is better to fail than to succeed.
  c The creators of the exhibit believe that people learn from failure.
  d Something that is imperfect can still be useful.

4 According to paragraph 4, what happened to make the items imperfect?
  a The artist made the imperfections on purpose.
  b Something damaged them after they were made.
  c A mistake made them all the wrong color.
  d Imperfect items are important in the artists' cultures.

5 The meaning of the word *process* in paragraph 3 is similar to
  a routine.
  b procedure.
  c result.
  d instruction.

6 According to paragraph 3, all of the following statements are true of the imperfect items EXCEPT:
  a Unusable items were rejected.
  b Imperfect small statues were accepted.
  c Imperfect coins were usable and accepted.
  d Imperfect items had no value.

7 The meaning of the word *deliberate* in paragraph 4 is similar to
  a intentional.
  b unintentional.
  c unsuccessful.
  d delicate.

4 Read the article again and match the causes with the effects.

1 In the process of making these items, something went wrong.
2 Some imperfect items were unusable.
3 Some imperfect items, like coins, were acceptable.
4 Some cultures think imperfection is acceptable.

  a People used them.
  b Artists made imperfect items on purpose.
  c They're imperfect.
  d The artists rejected them.

Less Than Perfect

1 Museums are famous for their great works of art. Perfect sculptures, paintings, and treasures from ancient times are what people expect to see. Usually. But one museum has an unusual exhibit of items that are imperfect. It's called "Less Than Perfect."

2 Some of the imperfect items are coins that are not circular, bottles that bend to one side, and ceramic pots that are thin on one side and thick on the other. These items are failures. Some objects in the exhibit are more than 2,000 years old, but others are more recent mistakes. They were found all over the world, and now are at the Kelsey Museum of Archaeology at the University of Michigan in the US.

3 There are two important parts to the exhibit. The first is "Failed Perfection." It includes imperfect bowls, glass, small statues, coins, and other objects. In the process of making these items, something went wrong, and the result was imperfections in the product. The artists had to reject some things because they were unsuccessful and unusable. For example, a bowl with a crack in it, or a bottle that formed without a bottom. But other imperfect items, such as small statues and coins with the image not in the center, were acceptable and people used them.

4 The second part is called "Deliberate Imperfection." With these items, the artists made them imperfect on purpose. This was often for cultural reasons. For example, some Japanese pottery from five hundred years ago has flaws* on purpose because of the idea that there is beauty in imperfection.

5 The museum shows these imperfect objects to make people think about what *perfect* meant to other cultures in different times. And to think about what people learned from these failures.

flaw *mistake, imperfection*

6C Unexpected Art

GRAMMAR Zero conditional

1 Listen and complete the sentences. 🎧 66

1 When you try hard, you _____.
2 If you learn to drive, you _____ my car.
3 If you listen carefully, you _____ a lot.
4 If you don't study, you _____ the test.
5 When people exercise, their health _____.
6 When I buy fruit at the farmer's market, it _____ better.
7 When I watch movies in English, I _____ new vocabulary.
8 When he doesn't get enough sleep, he _____ very rude.

2 Match the phrases to make complete sentences.

1 If you fail, ___
2 When you iron your clothes, ___
3 When Emilio cooks, ___
4 If a player scores a goal, ___
5 When you come to my house, ___
6 If she drinks too much coffee, ___
7 When the baby cries, ___
8 When his phone rings, ___

a they look better.
b you can meet my family.
c Jun looks to see who is calling before he answers.
d try again until you succeed.
e she feels nervous.
f the food is very spicy.
g the game is over.
h his mother picks him up.

3 Complete the sentences.

a painting party is	If someone needs a break,
if the painting isn't perfect,	they laugh about it with a friend
they often share a photo of it online	

If you want your friends to spend time together,
(1) _____ a good idea. It's creative and fun.
A teacher gives instructions, but nobody's work is a failure.
When people make mistakes, (2) _____. They
accept imperfections. (3) _____ she can have
something to eat or drink and chat with others. It is a party after
all. When people finish a picture, (4) _____.
And (5) _____ they still share it!

4 Read the paragraph. Find six errors and correct them.

If you use social media be careful about what you post. For
example, when you are posting photos, think about the
other people in the photos. If they don't want the photo
online, you shouldn't to post it. If you post comments don't
write anything inappropriate or unkind. When you receive a
friend request from someone you don't know don't accept
it. If you want to keep your information private, you can to
change the settings. And when you are online too much,
you take a break for a day or two.

5 Listen and underline the clause in which you hear rising intonation. 🎧 67

1 If you want to relax, you should watch a good movie.
2 When you're in a movie theater, you can forget other things and enjoy the movie.
3 If you like movies, go to the film festival.
4 When you're at a film festival, you should see several movies.
5 If you watch a movie in English, you can learn new vocabulary.
6 When you see a movie you like, you should tell your friends to see it.
7 When you see a movie you don't like, you should tell your friends not to see it.

6 Choose the correct words to complete the paragraph.

When you're in London, *take / taking* a walk through Harrod's food hall. It's a world of specialty food. Sometimes *when / if* you walk through the hall, you *can / can't* try samples, like a piece of chocolate or a taste of meat or cheese. The large hall and the foods are beautiful. Just looking is almost as good as eating. But, if you have a camera, *shouldn't / don't* use it. Photography is not allowed.

7 Put the words in order to make sentences. In sentences where the comma is not present, then the result clause comes first.

1 Lima / neighborhood / to / you / the / go / when / to / go / Miraflores

_____

2 phone / if / turn off / your / relax, / want / you / to

_____

3 stand / I / take / always / when / the / I / bus,

_____

4 comes / news / watches / my / when / he / father / home, / the

_____

5 I / my / family / coffee / I / make / get up / for / when

_____

6 a / if / make / are / sandwich / you / hungry, / you / can

_____

7 try / if / flavor/ ice cream, / like / you / this / should / you

_____

8 you / you / test, / talk / a / test / if / fail / during / the

_____

8 Complete the sentences using the zero conditional with your own ideas.

1 If you don't try to speak English,

_____

_____

2 When you travel overseas, _____

_____

3 If you visit my city, _____

4 When you visit my country, _____

_____

5 If you like art, _____

_____

6 When you don't succeed, _____

_____

7 If you like something, _____

_____

8 When you don't like something, _____

6D Teach girls bravery, not perfection

TEDTALKS

AUTHENTIC LISTENING SKILLS

1 Complete the extracts from the TED Talk with words or phrases that mark contrast. Then listen to check your answers. 🎧 **68**

1 For years, I had existed safely behind the scenes in politics as a fundraiser, as an organizer, _____, I always wanted to run.

2 She had never lost a race, and no one had really even run against her in a Democratic primary. _____, this was my way to make a difference, to disrupt the status quo.

3 The polls, _____, told a very different story.

4 We have to show them that they will be loved and accepted not for being perfect _____ for being courageous.

WATCH ▶

2 Complete the sentences with the correct words.

accepted	brave	failed	failure
perfect	risk	socialize	trial and error

1 This is not a talk about the importance of _____.

2 It was the first time in my entire life that I had done something that was truly _____, where I didn't worry about being _____.

3 Most girls are taught to avoid _____ and failure.

4 It's often said in Silicon Valley, no one even takes you seriously unless you've had two _____ start-ups.

5 Coding, it's an endless process of _____, of trying to get the right command in the right place, with sometimes just a semicolon making the difference between success and failure.

6 We have to show them that they will be loved and _____ not for being perfect but for being courageous.

7 We have to _____ our girls to be comfortable with imperfection, and we've got to do it now.

3 Put the sentences in order.

_____ The coding teachers notice that the girls feel they have to be perfect.

_____ Saujani ran for Congress but was unsuccessful.

_____ Saujani wants girls to learn to code and to be comfortable with imperfection.

_____ She started a company to teach girls to code.

_____ Saujani says that girls are taught not to take risks.

4 Choose the correct words to complete the sentences.

1 Writing computer code takes trial and error. It is *easy / difficult* to get it right at first.

2 Girls often *delete / correct* their code when it has mistakes.

3 Boys usually say, "There's a problem with *me / my code.*"

4 Girls usually say, "There's a problem with *me / my computer.*"

5 Good coders are *perfect / brave.*

6 Saujani thinks we should *be comfortable with / fight* imperfection.

VOCABULARY IN CONTEXT

5 Complete the sentences with the correct words.

courageous	negotiate		potential	ran
struggling	supportive network			

1 She _____ for Congress but she didn't win.

2 People have to learn to _____. It's a skill that takes practice.

3 When students move to another country to study, it's hard because they don't have a _____ in the new place.

4 My teacher says I have the _____ to do better in this class.

5 It's more important to be _____ than perfect.

6 I'm really _____ with this assignment.

6E Giving Advice

SPEAKING

Useful language

Giving advice

If someone asks for advice, use these expressions.

When you don't understand something in class, *you should* ask your teacher for help.

If you need more math practice, *try* downloading a math app.

Why don't you…

The best time to give advice is when someone asks for it. If someone hasn't asked, but you want to give advice, be polite and use these expressions.

If the computer isn't working, *you might want to try* re-starting it.

I can see you don't have a phone signal. *I got a signal near the window, and* that may work for you.

I'm not sure, but I think this door is locked after 6:00. *You may/might* need to use the side entrance.

1 Complete the exchanges with words and phrases from the Useful language box. Some items may have more than one answer. Then listen and check your answers. 🎧 **69**

1 A: How can I get better at this video game?
B: _____ watch some online tutorials?

2 A: I'm really worried about cooking dinner for everyone this weekend.
B: _____ you aren't confident in the kitchen, _____ asking someone for help.

3 A: I always know exactly where I'm going.
B: _____ this is the wrong way. _____ need to go back to the main road.

4 A: This is useless. I can't do it!
B: _____ you're not sure about the answer, _____ checking it with someone.

5 A: Oh no! I'm going to look so stupid. Everyone else is so much better than me!
B: You look a little nervous. I think about my breathing when I'm nervous, and _____.

6 A: I've just failed my driving test. What am I going to do?
B: _____ you don't succeed at something, _____ try to do it again.

2 Listen to the sentences in Activity 1. Underline the words that have a higher pitch. Listen to the example. 🎧 **70**

Example: *A: There's <u>nothing</u> to do!*
B: If you're <u>bored</u>, you <u>could</u> help me clean the house.

3 Read the advice. Decide if the other person asked for the advice (Y) or not (N).

1 If the homework is too difficult, try asking for some help. _____

2 If the bus is late, you might want to try checking the app. _____

3 Why don't you Google it? _____

4 I found a great price when I searched online, that might work for you. _____

5 I'm not sure, but I think you need to reserve a seat. You might want to check. _____

6 When you go to South America, you should visit Machu Picchu. _____

4 Read the situations and make notes about what advice you would offer. Use the useful language. Then listen to the sample answers and compare your ideas. 🎧 **71**

1 You are waiting at a bus stop. Some tourists are talking about where they can go for lunch.

2 An online friend talks to you about her problems with her brother/sister. He/She is often unkind and they argue a lot.

3 You reply to a post on social media asking what music is popular in your country.

4 Some people visiting your town are planning to go to the local museum tomorrow, but that's the day when it's usually closed.

WRITING An advice blog

1 Read the advice blog. Label the sections.

a conclusion	b problem	c topic
d solution 1	e solution 2	f solution 3

_____ It's good to have goals.

_____ You might have personal goals, like traveling or learning a new language, and, of course, academic and professional goals are also important. But goals can cause problems, too. Some people worry so much about their goals that they forget about everything else. This can be unhealthy. If you have a goal that is taking up all of your time, here is some advice that might help.

_____ Think about what really matters in your life, for example, your family and your friends. While you are working on your goal, make sure you still see the people who care about you. Focusing on your goals and nothing else could make you very lonely.

_____ It may sound obvious, but don't forget to eat well and sleep enough at night. If you're putting all of your energy into your goals so that you miss meals and go to bed too late, you could get sick. Take care of your health and well-being!

_____ Keep a positive attitude about your goals, but try to have another plan in case something goes wrong. It's normal to feel disappointed when we don't reach our goals, but it's important not to become too upset. After all, there are always other things you can do.

_____ Remember, goals are great, but we all need a healthy balance between living well and working toward our goals.

2 Read the advice blog in Activity 1 again. Are the statements true (T) or false (F)?

1 The blogger doesn't think that people should have goals. ___
2 According to the blog, it's a problem when we focus too much on our goals. ___
3 The blogger advises people not to spend too much time with their family and friends. ___
4 The blog reminds people to eat and sleep well while working on their goals. ___
5 When we don't reach our goals, we shouldn't feel disappointed. ___
6 The blogger's conclusion is that it's best to have a balanced approach to our goals. ___

3 Complete the problem and solution text with the correct words or phrases.

a problem	advice	costs nothing	don't worry
for free	good news	no problem	too expensive
way too much	wonderful		

Money gives us the freedom to do many things. But not having enough money is (1) _____ that many of us live with. However, there is (2) _____. Follow this (3) _____ , and soon you'll find yourself enjoying the things you thought you couldn't afford!

All your friends are members of a gym, and they go to lots of cool classes. The fees too high for you? (4) _____. Exercising in nature (5) _____, and anyway is more fun. Invite your friends to join you for a run on the beach or a bike ride in the park. Have fun!

You love the theater, but tickets cost (6) _____? No problem. Volunteer, or get a part-time job working at a theater a couple of evenings a week. The work isn't difficult, and you'll get to see the shows (7) _____. Enjoy!

Everyone is talking about this beautiful restaurant in town, right? You want to go, but it's (8)_____. No problem. Most restaurants offer special deals that don't cost very much, especially in the middle of the week. Check it out!

So, if you don't have much money, (9) _____. It's still possible to do many (10) _____ things!

4 Choose one of the problems.

Everyone I know is really into sports. I mean, everyone in my family and all my friends either watch sports, or play sports, or both. The problem is that I have absolutely no interest in sports. I find them boring. What can I do? —_Tomas_	_So I got my driver's license last month, which is great. The problem is now everyone expects me to drive them everywhere! I don't mind helping sometimes, but my friends are always asking me to take them places. What should I do?_ —_Yumi_

Write a paragraph offering advice for one of the problems. Suggest at least three solutions.

- confirm what the problem is
- establish why it is a problem
- offer some solutions
- end with a concluding sentence

5 Write about the following topic.

> Guido has very good neighbors, but one drops by to visit much too often, and another parks her car on Guido's lawn.
>
> What are the problems and solutions?

Give reasons for your answer and include any relevant examples from your own knowledge or experience.

Write at least 250 words.

Review

1 Re-order the words to make sentences.

1 the / for / gift / shopping / girlfriend / perfect / for / my / I'm

_____

2 the / didn't / failed / and / study / he / test

_____

3 movies / actor / was / the / two / in / unsuccessful

_____

4 today / is / perfect / weather / the

_____

5 in / is / nature / perfection / there

_____

6 made / he / the / a / pie / success / was

_____

7 it / product / fix / this / claims / skin imperfections / will

_____

8 afraid / to / fail / be / don't

_____

2 Match the word or phrase to its meaning.

1 courageous
2 negotiate
3 potential
4 ran
5 struggling
6 supportive network

a discuss and make compromises
b people that care about you and help you
c ability
d tried to win an election
e having difficulty
f brave, not afraid

3 Use the prompts to write complete sentences.

1 turn off / phones / in school

_____

2 not / wear / sneakers / restaurant

_____

3 need to / charge / phone

_____

4 buy tickets / for / before Saturday

_____

5 not / use phone / in

_____

6 go home / before / dark

_____

7 be / 18 / to

_____

8 not text / teacher

_____

4 Complete the descriptions with your own ideas.

Example: If something is perfect, _people like it_.

1 When someone is confident,

_____

2 If a sports team is successful,

_____

3 If the students are hard-working,

_____

4 When a person is lazy on the weekend,

_____

5 I accept help from others when

_____

6 She feels brave when

_____

7 A project fails when

_____

8 When I don't succeed at something,

_____

5 Write a paragraph to a student who started learning English recently. In your response, use modals, the zero conditional, and vocabulary from the unit.

_____
_____
_____
_____
_____
_____
_____
_____
_____
_____
_____
_____
_____
_____
_____
_____
_____
_____
_____
_____

7 Tell Me What You Eat

7A Food and Flavors from Around the World

VOCABULARY Foods, drinks, and flavors

1 **Review** Listen. Match the descriptions to the images. 🎧 **72**

a

b

c

d

e

f

1 _____   4 _____
2 _____   5 _____
3 _____   6 _____

2 **Review** Listen again. Complete the sentences with one word in each space. 🎧 **72**

1 The meal they are talking about is _____.
   He had juice with this meal today.
2 She drank _____ and ate
   _____ this morning.
3 He's having some _____ and a
   _____ for _____ today.
4 He's going to have _____ and salad for
   _____.
5 She usually has _____ and
   _____ in the evening.
6 She doesn't think it's a good idea to have
   _____ later because of the
   _____.

3 For each item, write one word from the list that describes it.

dessert	drink	meat	salty
sour	spicy	vegetable	

1 lemon _____
2 tomato _____
3 curry _____
4 potato chip _____
5 tea _____
6 ice cream _____
7 chicken _____

4 Complete the sentences with the correct words.

1 I want to cook something spicy. Do we have any
   c_____ p_____?
2 The s_____ in our garden are small, dark red, and
   very sweet.
3 Sandwiches often come with f_____ f_____
   at restaurants, but you should order a salad instead.
   They are less salty and much better for you!
4 A_____ grow on trees, and they can be red, yellow,
   or green. They can also be sweet or sour.
5 Many children don't like the flavor of v_____.
   They prefer s_____ desserts like i_____
   c_____.
6 She likes beef and chicken, but she can't eat fish or
   s_____. Seafood makes her sick.
7 Ch_____ o_____ is a popular ingredient
   that is used in many desserts, and even hot drinks, but
   without sugar in it, it is actually quite b_____.

5 Choose the correct words to complete the sentences.

1 French fries are made from *potatoes / tomatoes*.
2 Mexicans eat a lot of *spice / spicy* food.
3 Strawberries are *sweet / salty*.
4 Many people enjoy the *flavor / snack* of coffee.
5 Coffee and tea are *sour / bitter* before you add sugar and milk.
6 Ice cream is a popular *drink / dessert* all around the world.
7 Apples are a very common *fruit / vegetable*.
8 Italian-style *pasta / lemon* with meat and tomato sauce is
   very popular in countries like the US and Argentina.
9 *Shrimp / Chicken* comes from the ocean.

6 Listen. Choose the correct description. 🎧 **73**

1 a She's cooking Indian food.
  b She's making a fruit salad.
  c She's eating a salty snack.

2 a He's going to buy a snack.
  b He needs an ingredient to make dinner.
  c He wants a hot drink.

3 a She doesn't like very spicy food.
  b She loves her friend's cooking.
  c She wants some more chicken.

4 a She's preparing food for a party.
  b She doesn't eat meat.
  c She's ordering sandwiches at a cafe.

5 a He doesn't like the lunch dishes.
  b He's trying to choose a dessert.
  c He's not very hungry.

6 a She's looking for the meat section.
  b She's looking for the fruit section.
  c She's looking for the snack section.

7 Extension Complete the crossword.

Across
1 cheap and quick meal, for example, a burger and French fries (2 words)
5 bad for you
8 cooked over fire
9 cooked in hot water
10 cooked in hot oil

Down
1 very cold, like ice
2 tastes very good
3 really bad
4 it makes your food spicy (2 words)
6 like vegetables picked from the garden this morning
7 very large

8 Extension Choose the correct words to complete the text from the multiple choice items below. Write the letter of the correct word on the line.

Let's face it—many people today have a pretty (1) ___ diet. Lots of people don't take time to eat a good lunch with friends or family. Instead, they get (2) ___, which is cheap and often fried or covered with cheese, and they eat it quickly in their cars. They drink soda or coffee drinks full of sugar. After work, they are too tired to cook, so they heat up some (3) ___ meals from the supermarket. Or they go out to restaurants, where they are served a (4) ___ amount of food—and there is often a big dessert after the meal! All of this is (5) ___ for the body.

However, things are starting to change. More and more people are interested in changing their habits. They are buying (6) ___ fruits, vegetables, meat, and eggs from local farms. They're drinking water instead of soda. They're looking for restaurants that serve normal-sized dishes with interesting (7) ___ and local ingredients. They are discovering that home-cooked meals (8) ___, and that (9) ___ foods are lighter and healthier than (10) ___ foods.

1 a healthy
  b spicy
  c unhealthy
2 a a home-cooked meal
  b fast food
  c fresh vegetables
3 a frozen
  b amazing
  c boiled
4 a fresh
  b frozen
  c huge
5 a terrible
  b delicious
  c natural

6 a frozen
  b fresh
  c boiled
7 a amounts
  b flavors
  c delicious
8 a taste terrible
  b smell bad
  c taste amazing
9 a grilled
  b salty
  c fried
10 a boiled
  b fried
  c sweet

PRONUNCIATION

9 Listen and choose the words you hear. Then practice saying the sentences with both words. 🎧 **74**

1 Are you going to *taste / waste* that food?
2 I think this dish needs more *rice / spice*.
3 *Peas / Bees* are very important on the farm.
4 Can you please pass me that *meat / wheat*?
5 A great way to relax is to *bike / bake*.
6 I don't like the smell of this *beef / leaf*.
7 He made the chicken and vegetables in a *curry / hurry*.
8 I got the recipe from a *cook / book*.

LISTENING

10 Listen and answer the questions. 🎧 **75**

1 What is a potluck dinner?
  a Everyone cooks the meal together.
  b Everyone brings a dish to the dinner.
  c Everyone tries to guess what the food is.

2 What is the man planning on bringing?
  a a cheesecake
  b a dessert
  c a curry

3 What does the woman need for her dish?
  a organic honey
  b cheesecake
  c hot peppers

4 What does the woman think might be funny?
  a if she isn't able to get the organic honey
  b if he doesn't warn people about the spices
  c if they bring the same dish to the dinner

5 What is the woman definitely going to do?
  a make a dessert
  b make a cheesecake
  c make something spicy

6 What is the woman not sure about?
  a if she'll be able to eat all the spicy foods
  b if other people are bringing dishes to the dinner
  c what she'll make if she doesn't get the honey

11 Listen to the speaker and decide what his philosophy about life is. 🎧 **76**

  a Don't regret the mistakes you've made.
  b Be kind to everyone you meet.
  c Find something you enjoy and do it.
  d Keep calm and carry on.

12 Listen again. Choose the correct answers. 🎧 **76**

1 What has the young man been wondering about?
  a if he should work in a restaurant or not
  b if he should go to college or not
  c if he should ask his parents for money or not

2 Why does he think some people go to college?
  a because they feel like they're supposed to
  b because that's the best way to get a good job
  c because they'll be disappointed if they don't

3 How long has he worked at the local restaurant?
  a since last summer
  b he hasn't yet
  c for three summers

4 What is he doing this summer?
  a working at the restaurant
  b going to culinary school
  c he still isn't sure

5 How long does the culinary program last?
  a 8 weeks
  b 2 years
  c 18 months

6 What is he going to do if he isn't accepted to culinary school?
  a think about a different career
  b continue to work toward his career goal
  c apply to a university or college

7 Why does he feel so lucky?
  a because he has a good job in a restaurant
  b because he is going to a culinary school
  c because he knows what he wants to do

GRAMMAR Predictions and arrangements

13 Complete the sentences with the correct form of *will* and the verb in parentheses.

1 We _____ (not eat) all of this food!
2 The tomatoes _____ (be) ripe to eat in July.
3 Nonno's Pizza, a new restaurant, _____ (open) in two weeks.
4 I _____ (call) the restaurant and make a reservation.
5 The sushi delivery _____ (arrive) in 30 minutes.
6 Turn down the heat, or the sauce _____ (burn).
7 Friday's newspaper _____ (print) a review of Finn's Café.
8 We _____ (not have) enough time to make a salad.

14 Put the words in the correct order to make questions.

1 we / have / a / Sarah / party / this / will / year / big / for
_____

2 family / invite / of / friends / we / her / all / and / will
_____

3 the / will / food / parents / our / prepare / help
_____

4 help / Ana / with / will / decorations / the
_____

5 invitations / will / by / send / email / the / we
_____

6 will / cake / bake / a / David
_____

15 Use the prompts to write predictions that are true for you. Use *will*, *going to, may,* or *might.*

1 speak English _____
2 travel to _____
3 meet _____
4 try _____
5 know _____
6 In 5 years, I _____
7 In 10 years, _____

16 Complete the sentences about the "superfood" kale with the correct verb forms.

1 One serving of kale *will give / is going to give* you more calcium than a large glass of milk.
2 Eating kale *going to add / will add* fiber, protein, omega-3s, and vitamins and minerals to your diet.
3 One cup of kale *are going to have / will have* only 33 calories and tons of vitamins, minerals, and protein.
4 If you buy kale, it *won't to be / isn't going to be* expensive.
5 You can use kale to make lots of things. *You going to want / You'll want* to try it in a smoothie, a salad, a side dish—or baked as a chip!
6 Adding kale to your diet *won't to cause / is not going to cause* medical problems.
7 If you travel to Scotland, Kenya, or Portugal, you *will seeing / are going to see* kale on the menu.
8 The average person in other places *going to eating / will eat* only two to three cups of kale every year.

17 Complete the sentences with the correct form of the verbs in parentheses. There may be more than one correct answer.

1 Tonight, the chef _____ (prepare) his favorite meal, Spaghetti Bolognese, for us.
2 The sous chef _____ (help) by chopping onions, carrots, celery, and tomatoes and gathering the garlic, rosemary, basil, and oregano.
3 The chef _____ (start) by boiling the spaghetti in salted water.
4 Then he _____ (begin) cooking the sauce.
5 He _____ (heat) olive oil in a pan and then cook the onion, carrot, celery, garlic, and rosemary for about ten minutes.
6 Then he _____ (stir) in the ground beef and cook it until it's brown.
7 He _____ (add) canned tomatoes, basil, oregano, tomato puree, and fresh tomatoes.
8 He _____ (cook) the sauce for about an hour and create a thick, rich sauce.
9 Finally, he _____ (combine) the cooked spaghetti and sauce.
10 He _____ (serve) the spaghetti with grated Parmesan cheese.

7B Urban Farms: The Future of Food?

VOCABULARY BUILDING

1 Complete each sentence using the correct form of the word in parentheses. Add the suffix *-er, -ment,* or *-ance,* and make changes to spelling where necessary.

1 What might be some of the consequences of the _____ (disappear) of farming as a way of life?

2 Where will our food come from if fewer people decide to become _____ (farm) in the future?

3 The _____ (develop) of urban and vertical farms will be a big step toward helping feed people in the future.

4 Being able to grow food indoors for millions of people would be a tremendous _____ (accomplish).

5 Urban farming is an exciting field that brings together plant scientists, architects, urban _____ (plan), engineers, and economists.

READING

2 Read the article and answer the questions.

1 Why is urban farming an important development for the future?

a It's important to control conditions such as carbon dioxide, humidity, and light.

b According to the U.N., 6.5 billion people will live in cities by 2050.

c because stores don't produce the food they sell

d If farming as a way of life disappears, urban farms will help feed people in cities.

2 What are some advantages of urban or vertical farms?

a In the near future, twice as many people will live in cities as today.

b Traditional farming as a way of life is slowly disappearing.

c You can control light and water, and you don't have to worry about weather or insects.

d A personal food computer keeps track of conditions such as carbon dioxide levels, humidity, and light intensity.

3 How is aeroponic farming different from traditional farming?

a Both aeroponic and traditional farmers need to worry about insects, weather, and light conditions.

b Engineers, architects, urban planners, economists, and plant scientists all work together on aeroponic farms.

c Unlike traditional farms, aeroponic farms can control growing conditions 365 days a year.

d Aeroponic farms will be one way you'll get at least some of your food in the future.

4 How do plants in a food computer receive nutrients?

a A food computer is a climate-controlled box.

b Sensors in a food computer keep track of humidity and light.

c Aeroponically grown plants don't need sunlight.

d They're fed by a mist that includes necessary minerals.

5 Why are vertical farms able to provide food right where it's needed?

a because plants in vertical farms don't need sunlight

b because vertical farms can be located in cities

c because not all of our food comes from stores

d because vertical farms work 365 days a year

3 Choose the correct heading for each paragraph from the list below.

1 Paragraph 1	**a** Urban farms of the future
2 Paragraph 2	**b** Who will feed the future?
3 Paragraph 3	**c** Aeroponic farming
4 Paragraph 4	**d** Aeroponics and you!
5 Paragraph 5	**e** Personal "food computers"

4 Match the words to the definitions.

1 estimate ___	**a** a chemical substance found in nature
2 mineral ___	**b** a person who has scientific training and who designs and builds complex structures
3 root ___	
4 factory ___	
5 climate ___	**c** to make an informed guess
6 vertical ___	**d** the typical weather in a place
7 row ___	**e** going up and down rather than from side to side
8 engineer ___	**f** the part of a plant that grows below the ground
	g a building in which products are made
	h a group of objects arranged in a line

Urban Farms: The Future of Food?

1 Do you know where your food comes from? Does it matter to you? If you live in a city, you probably get most, if not all, of your food from stores. Of course you know that stores don't produce the food they sell. Farms do. But did you know that farming as a way of life is slowly disappearing? The United Nations estimates that by 2050, 6.5 billion people will live in cities. (That's about twice as many as today.) If fewer and fewer people become farmers, where is our food going to come from?

2 Caleb Harper, a National Geographic Explorer, has an idea. Caleb thinks that people should grow food near the places they live, and not just on traditional farms. He's part of a new movement that hopes to see "urban farms" and "vertical* farms" in cities in the not-too-distant future. Caleb's organization is the CityFARM research group. CityFARM brings together engineers, architects, urban planners, economists, and plant scientists to study alternatives to traditional farms.

3 One of the tools Caleb is interested in developing is what he calls a "personal food computer." A food computer is a small box with plants inside it. The food computer has sensors* that measure conditions such as carbon dioxide levels, humidity, and the amount of light. There's no dirt. The plants get nutrients* through a mist, a fine spray of water, that has minerals added in.

4 This type of farming, in which plant roots are fed by mist and not grown in soil, is called aeroponics. Now picture a type of aeroponic food computer that's as big as a warehouse*. In here, plants grow without soil or sunlight. All of the plants are fed aeroponically (by mist) and the climate is controlled. There's no risk of storms, cold weather, or droughts. Insects can't harm the plants. The system works 365 days a year, day and night. That's more or less what a vertical* farm is like.

5 Because vertical farms can be built in cities, inside of old warehouses or factories, or even on top of schools, they can provide food right where it's needed. Whether it's a personal food computer designed to grow your favorite vegetables in your home, or a vertical farm in an urban apartment building, aeroponic farming will probably be one of the ways you get at least some of your food in the future.

vertical *up and down instead of side to side*
sensors *a devices that responds to heat, light, pressure, etc.*
nutrients *substances that plants, animals, and people need to live and grow*
warehouse *a large building used for storing goods*

7C A Taste of Honey

GRAMMAR First conditional

1 Listen and complete the sentences. 🎧 78

1 _____ you go hiking in Arizona, _____ need to wear sunscreen.

2 You _____ lose your work _____ you don't save your files every ten minutes.

3 _____ you water your plants every week, _____ be healthy and beautiful.

4 I _____ get my driver's license in the fall _____ I take driving lessons this summer.

5 You _____ wear your blue suit _____ you go to your cousin's birthday.

6 _____ I leave my hat by the pool, my sister _____ get it for me.

7 It _____ be difficult to do well on your exam _____ you play video games all afternoon.

2 Listen. Complete each sentence with the correct word or punctuation. 🎧 79

1 _____ you go hiking in the desert _____ you might see some interesting wildlife.

2 I might have to take summer school _____ I fail the exam.

3 I may go rock climbing _____ I visit Phoenix.

4 _____ you stay out on the beach too long _____ you could get a sunburn.

5 _____ we don't pay the rent _____ our landlord may be upset.

6 I may eat tacos _____ I go to that new Mexican restaurant.

3 Check the sentence in each pair that is more certain.

1 _____ If the apartment is dirty, Lara may clean it.

  _____ When the apartment is dirty, Lara will clean it.

2 _____ He will do yoga and meditation when he is upset.

  _____ If he is upset, he might do yoga and meditation.

3 _____ When you learn to swim, you'll go to the pool more often.

  _____ You may go to the pool more often if you learn to swim.

4 _____ If you listen to this music, you may love it!

  _____ You'll love this music when you listen to it!

5 _____ Khalid won't come with me when I go to the movies on Saturday.

  _____ Khalid might not come with me if I go to the movies on Saturday.

6 _____ When I go to Canada, I won't visit Toronto.

  _____ I might not visit Toronto if I go to Canada.

7 _____ When you go to the meeting with your teacher, she'll help you with your paper.

  _____ If you go to the meeting with your teacher, she may help you with your paper.

8 _____ I could have a banana and some tea if I get hungry on my flight.

  _____ When I get hungry on my flight, I'll have a banana and some tea.

4 Choose the correct words to complete the sentences. There may be more than one correct answer.

1 *If / When* you like Spanish food, you might want to make a *tortilla*.

2 *If / When* you want to make one, you'll need a lot of eggs.

3 *If / When* you go to the store, you'll also need to buy potatoes, olive oil, and onion.

4 *If / When* you cut the onion, it *might / will* make you cry.

5 When the olive oil is hot, it *may / will* be time to add the onion and potato.

6 *If / When* the onions and potato are cooked, you'll need to add the egg.

7 When you flip the tortilla, you *might / will* drop it. Be careful!

8 *If / When* you eat it, you might want to serve a small salad or some bread as well.

9 *If / When* you're trying to lose weight, you won't want to eat too much!

5 Choose the correct option to complete the sentences.

1 I *eat / ate* hummus and tabbouleh when I want to be really healthy.

2 If I learn to swim, *I'll go / I'll to go* to the pool every day.

3 If we go to the city center for the game, we *could / if* go to that new restaurant for lunch.

4 I *won't / could* buy any cheese when I go to the store.

5 If you go outside tonight, you might *see / seeing* the full moon.

6 Remember you could call your cousin *won't / if* you need help.

7 If you drive too fast, you may *get / got* a ticket.

8 When it's raining tomorrow, you *might want / will want* to go see a movie.

6 For each question, complete the second sentence so that it means the same as the first. Use no more than three words.

1 I may win the contest, and if that happens, I will get a prize.

_____ I win the contest,

_____ get a prize.

2 It's possible that you will not go to the party with Mary, and if that happens, she will be upset.

If you _____ go to the party with Mary,

_____ be upset.

3 Sometimes I go to bed at 8:00, and when I do, I am happy when I wake up.

_____ I go to bed at 8:00,

I _____ up happy.

4 We are going to the beach in July, and when we do, it's possible I will go diving.

_____ we go to the beach in July, I

_____ go diving.

5 He could be late, and if he is, he'll call to tell you.

_____ he's _____ to be

late, he'll _____ to tell you.

6 We may see the play on Saturday, but if we don't see it, we won't have a chance to see it again.

If we _____ see the play on Saturday, we

_____ it at all.

7 I could read the lesson ahead of time, and if I do, I might answer more questions in class.

I _____ answer more questions in class

_____ I read the lesson ahead of time.

7 Read each question. Choose the correct answer.

1 When will you pay me back if I lend you money?
   a If you lend me money, I will pay you back next week.
   b I might pay you back next week when you are lending me money.

2 When she goes to Paris, what will she do?
   a She might visit the Eiffel Tower when she's in Paris.
   b If she goes to Paris, she may visit the Eiffel Tower.

3 If you buy a new car, will it cost a lot of money?
   a I won't buy a new car if I may not have a lot of money.
   b If I buy a new car, it may cost a lot of money.

4 Did you talk to Rob today?
   a No, I didn't. But I may speak with him later if I go to science club.
   b No, I didn't. When I go to science club I won't speak with him.

5 Will your mother be annoyed if you don't go on vacation with your parents this year?
   a Yes, if we wouldn't go, she could be annoyed.
   b Yes, if we don't go, she'll be annoyed.

6 When you walk along the river this afternoon, will you bring a book to read?
   a Yes, I may bring a book when I walk along the river.
   b Yes, if I bring a book, I will walk along the river.

7 Did you mow your yard yet this year?
   a Yes, when it's sunny and warm last week, we could need to mow it.
   b No, but if it's sunny and warm next week, we may need to mow it.

8 Complete the sentences with your own ideas using the first conditional.

1 If I eat a lot of junk food,

_____ .

2 When I have time to cook dinner,

_____ .

3 If I don't have time to cook,

_____ .

4 I go to restaurants

_____ .

5 When I want something sweet,

_____ .

6 If I eat dinner with my family,

_____ .

7 When I eat with my friends,

_____ .

7D The global food waste scandal

TEDTALKS

AUTHENTIC LISTENING SKILLS

1 Listen to each extract. Choose the correct answer. 🎧 80

1 What do you think Stuart is going to talk about next?
   a He will explain his life story.
   b He will explain surplus.
   c He will explain why people get hungry.

2 What do you think Stuart is going to talk about next?
   a why he likes to shop at big supermarkets
   b what he found was being thrown away
   c the things he bought at the supermarket

3 What do you think Stuart is going to talk about next?
   a why biscuits are delicious
   b how biscuits are made
   c how biscuits connect to food waste

4 What do you think Stuart is going to talk about next?
   a how supermarkets are a part of wasting food
   b why supermarkets are doing a great job
   c why people should shop at supermarkets

5 What do you think Stuart is going to talk about next?
   a how people should get jobs as farmers
   b how farmers waste food
   c how farmers are losing their jobs

WATCH ▶

2 Choose the correct words to complete the sentences.

1 Stuart believes the solution to food waste is to simply *sit down and eat* / *throw away* food.

2 The wasted food that Stuart is talking about is *rotten* / *good, fresh* food.

3 People *cut down forests* / *make more supermarkets* to grow and farm more food.

4 Food goes to waste even before it leaves *the fields* / *people's houses*.

5 Corporations need to *grow their own food* / *tell people* what they are throwing away.

6 There are 13,000 slices of fresh bread coming out of factories in *one year* / *one day*.

3 Circle the things that Stuart says contribute to food waste.

1 the public
2 hungry people
3 animal food
4 the planet
5 farmers
6 corporations
7 supermarkets
8 lack of refrigeration

4 Match the words to the correct paraphrased line from the talk.

1 depend on ___
2 crust ___
3 unacceptable ___
4 symbol ___
5 hobby ___
6 very large quantity ___
7 demonstrate ___

a Food is being wasted by **an enormous amount**.
b These biscuits **represent** the global food supply.
c I need **to show** you where the food ends up.
d I inspect bins **in my free time**.
e Who eats the **first and last slice** of bread in a loaf?
f We throw away food that hungry people **need**.
g We can stop food waste if we say that **it isn't OK**.

VOCABULARY IN CONTEXT

5 Complete the sentences with the correct words.

global	households	invested
resources	tackle	

1 Stuart wants us to imagine that the nine biscuits that he found in the bin represent the _____ food supply.

2 He thinks people who live in most _____ don't eat the crust—that slice at the first and last end of each loaf.

3 The farmer has _____ 16,000 pounds in growing spinach.

4 He says people have the power to stop this awful waste of _____.

5 The global quest to _____ food waste has started.

7E What's it like?

SPEAKING

1 Listen and complete the sentences. 🎧 **81**

A: What are we going to do to celebrate the end of the class?

B: (1) _____ go bowling?

C: Maybe, but not everyone likes it.

A: (2) _____ a Hollywood party?

B: What's that?

A: (3) _____ film party where everyone dresses up as celebrities or movie characters.

C: That's a great idea. And a few of us are DJs, so we can put some music together.

B: We'll have plenty of music.

A: And (4) _____ popcorn… and nachos to eat.

C: Do you put meat on your nachos?

A: I make nachos with corn chips, guacamole, chili con carne, sour cream and cheese. So
(5) _____, a little
(6) _____, and (7) _____
with the cream too. (8) _____!

B: Yeah, (9) _____ party food.

A: And (10) _____ lots of people because you use the chips like a spoon, so you don't need knives and forks.

C: That sounds great.

B: (11) _____ the chili at my house.

A: And we'll need lots of corn chips, so
(12) _____ them?

B: Great idea.

C: This party's going to be awesome!

2 Read the three situations below. What suggestions do you have for them? For each situation, cover these three points:

- what is/are your idea(s)
- describe the places and things in your idea(s)
- explain why they are good in the situation

Make some notes for each situation. Use the speaking strategies.

1 A new friend is coming over to have dinner with your family. She's a vegetarian. What are you going to prepare for dinner?

2 An exchange student wants to know what is one of the most popular foods or meals in your country. Describe it for the student.

3 Your school wants to organize a campaign to reduce food waste in the cafeteria. What suggestions do you have?

3 Imagine that your friend has just started at a new school and wants to make new friends. Think of suggestions for things your friend can do to make friends. Make notes on your ideas. Use the Useful language. Then listen to a sample answer. 🎧 **82**

Below are some ideas to help you.

- sports
- drama group
- study group

WRITING A RESTAURANT REVIEW

1 Choose the correct words to complete the restaurant review.

Eastern Spice is a new *restaurant / coffee shop* on the corner of Main Street and Beech Road. It serves excellent Indian food, including curry, naan bread, and samosas. The chef grew up in northern India but has lived in the United States for many years. He helps his customers to understand how spicy the different *countries / dishes* are, and encourages everyone to try new *flavors / restaurants*. With only eight tables, the place is *huge / small* and extremely busy. However, I found it very noisy; the music was way too *loud / interesting*! Service is personal with *no / lots of* attention to detail, but a little too slow. *Prices / Menus* are reasonable… under $20 for two delicious courses! Eastern Spice is open from 6pm to midnight, Tuesday to Sunday. It doesn't open on Mondays. I *recommend / like* it for couples or a few friends, but not for large groups.

2 Read the restaurant review again. Then match the questions and answers.

1	What?	**a**	Main Street and Beech Road
2	What food?	**b**	6:00–12:00
3	Where?	**c**	A little slow
4	When?	**d**	Monday
5	Closed?	**e**	No
6	Service?	**f**	Eastern Spice
7	Expensive?	**g**	Yes
8	Recommended?	**h**	Indian dishes

3 Read the restaurant review. Choose the correct answers.

P&P is a popular Italian restaurant on Fairfield Avenue, next to the train station. Except Sundays, it's open every day from 12:30 to 10pm and, for dinner, you'll need a reservation. It's a large, casual place with lots of soft seats and brightly colored cushions. P&P stands for pizza and pasta, but they also serve salads and grilled meats. Everything is fresh and delicious! Compared to other Italian restaurants, prices are high, but I think it's worth it. The waiters and waitresses are very quick and efficient, and always smiling. I highly recommend it for celebrations and special occasions.

1 Where is the restaurant?
  a in the train station   **b** on Fairfield Avenue

2 Do you always need to make a reservation?
  a just on Sundays   **b** just for dinner

3 What is the atmosphere like?
  a large   **b** casual

4 What kind of food do they serve?
  a They serve a variety of dishes.   **b** They only serve pizza and pasta.

5 Is it expensive?
  a yes   **b** no

6 How would you describe the service?
  a too slow   **b** friendly

7 How would you describe the review?
  a mostly positive   **b** mostly negative

4 Write your own restaurant review. Choose one of the options below. Complete the notes with your ideas, then write your review.

TORO	ZEN
• Spanish restaurant	• Japanese restaurant
• 62 Summer Street	• Lavender Lane
• Mon–Fri, 6pm to _____	• Hours are _____
• Sat & Sun _____	• Chef is from Tokyo
• Dishes include paella and _____	• Atmosphere is stylish and _____
• Prices _____	• Dishes like sushi and _____
• Service is welcoming but _____	• Very expensive
• Atmosphere is _____	• Service is _____
• Recommend _____	• Recommend _____

5 Read the instructions.

- The graph below was created by a businessman. It shows the number of customers having meals at sit-down restaurants and fast-food restaurants in his hometown over a period of 30 years.
- Summarize the information by selecting and reporting the main features, and make comparisons where relevant.
- Write at least 150 words.

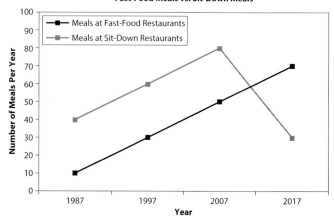

Fast-Food Meals vs. Sit-Down Meals

Review

1 Unscramble the letters to form the names of foods and drinks.

1 bleastgeve _____

2 fecfeo _____

3 otesmota _____

4 wrarbsetiser _____

5 keccinh _____

6 prihms _____

7 tapas _____

8 hacolcteo _____

2 Read the names of the recipes. Match them to the flavor descriptions.

1 Chili orange chicken with rice _____

2 Hot chocolate with hot peppers, sugar, and milk _____

3 Chocolate-covered potato chips _____

4 Shrimp with lemon pasta _____

5 Hot black tea with sugar and lemon _____

6 Strawberry pie and ice cream _____

7 Dark chocolate cake _____

8 French fries with cheese sauce _____

a It's a dessert that's sweet and a little bitter.

b It's a snack that's salty and sweet.

c It's a dinner with meat and fruit that's salty, sweet, and spicy.

d It's a dinner that's salty and a little bit sour.

e It's a warm, salty snack that isn't very light or healthy.

f It's a drink that's sweet and spicy.

g It's a drink that's bitter, sweet, and sour.

h It's a sweet fruit dessert.

3 Find and correct the errors.

I'm going to make pita bread with my friends tonight. (1) Its going to taste so good, because homemade bread is always better than bread from the supermarket.

First we need to get all the ingredients. (2) We are need yeast, oil, salt, flour, and water. (3) Jakob goes to buy the yeast and flour. I've already got the oil and salt.

(4) It taking a while to make the bread, but it's not complicated. (5) We're mixing the yeast and flour and add warm water. After 20 minutes, the dough will rise.

Next, we'll knead the dough and make it into a ball. (6) We put oil in a bowl so the dough doesn't stick as it rises. (7) That're going to take about two hours.

(8) Then we're going divide the dough into eight equal pieces and roll each one into a ball. (9) After half an hour, we are going rolling each ball out until it's a circle about 1/4 inch thick.

Finally, to cook the bread we need to heat a pan and add a little oil. (10) We are cooking the bread until it puffs up and turns brown. Then we'll flip it and cook the other side. When both sides are cooked, we'll have delicious bread to eat with dinner!

4 Re-order the words to make sentences.

1 the / they / exam / will / tomorrow / take

_____

2 when / goes / won't / to / library / , / she / return / her / she / the / books

_____

3 I / to / take / tomorrow / if / drive / , / will / don't / I / the / bus / school

_____

4 they're / to / tonight / play / going / together / music

_____

5 if / follow / might / directions / taste / his / cake / doesn't / , / the / he / bad

_____

6 won't / semester / next / take / a / Marla / math / class

_____

7 chairs / may / come / need / if / we / Anderson / and / Lea / to / extra / the / meeting / two

_____

5 Choose the correct option to complete the sentences.

1 If you take the time to learn the new material, *you'll / you won't* do well on the exam.

2 *I'll / I* may be home early if I catch the 4:37 train.

3 She *won't / don't* be in class if she has to go to the doctor's office.

4 When I *see / will see* my cousins next month, we might watch a movie together.

5 It *might / won't* rain when I go on my long bike ride tomorrow.

6 If you move to Rome, you might *learn / to learning* Italian.

7 She *may buy / could bought* some dessert if she has enough money.

8A   Why we buy

VOCABULARY   A product's life

1   **Review**   Label the photos.

department store	price tag	save money
shop online	shoppers	shopping mall

1 _____

2 _____

3 _____

4 _____

5 _____

6 _____

2   **Review**   Unscramble the words.

1   raktem _____

2   soctumre _____

3   pesxeivne _____

4   pahce _____

5   ripce _____

6   phogsinp lalm _____

7   pamdretnet trose _____

8   pends yenmo _____

3   **Review**   Complete the sentences with the correct words.

customer	department	expensive	mall	online
price	sale	save	spend	

1   When you buy something, you _____ money.

2   If you buy something at a low _____, then you _____ money.

3   If something is _____, it's not cheap.

4   A shopper is a _____ at a store.

5   If you don't like to go out shopping, you can shop _____.

6   There are usually lots of shops and a few large _____ stores at a shopping _____.

7   If something is not for _____, that means you can't buy it.

4   Add vowels to complete the vocabulary words.

1   m__n__f__ct__r__

2   m__t__r__ __l

3   __pt__ __n

4   __dv__rt__s__

5   r__c__cl__

6   thr__w __w__ __

7   d__s__gn

5   Match each word with its definition.

1   throw away ____   **a**   make in a factory

2   grow ____   **b**   what something is made of

3   recycle ____   **c**   choice

4   pick ____   **d**   put information about a product on TV, radio, in a magazine, or online to attract customers

5   manufacture ____

6   sell ____   **e**   get bigger

7   option ____   **f**   put in the trash

8   advertise ____   **g**   use something again

9   material ____   **h**   exchange a product for money

           i   choose

6 Choose the correct words to complete the sentences.

1 You shouldn't *throw away / pick* those shoes.
2 I want to *recycle / sell* my car.
3 Our company is *producing / growing* fast.
4 I'm not sure which pants to *pick / option*.
5 My friend *designs / manufactures* and makes her own dresses.
6 In a large shoe store, there are always many more *options / materials* to choose from.
7 What *manufacture / material* is that jacket made out of?
8 You know, you should really *recycle / throw away* more of your paper and plastic instead of throwing it away.

7 Complete the conversation. What does the salesperson say to the customer?

a Yes, but remember that these are all produced by hand. They're very special.
b It's made from recycled silk dresses from India.
c You can pick from any of these smaller bags here— they're all $80.
d All of our items are made by local artists.
e Yes, I know. We just opened last month, and we need to advertise more!
f I can sell it to you for $125.

A: Wow, that's a beautiful bag. Do you know who designed it?
B: 1 ____
A: What material is that? It looks very unusual.
B: 2 ____
A: Really? That's interesting! How much is it?
B: 3 ____
A: Oh, wow. Do you have any less expensive options?
B: 4 ____
A: Oh. Hmm. That's still a lot of money.
B: 5 ____
A: That's true. I like that they were not manufactured in a factory. I also like to support local businesses. I didn't even know this shop was here! I just saw it when I was walking by
B: 6 ____
A: Well I will tell all my friends about you. And… I'm sure my beautiful bag will get people's attention. I'll take that one with the pink and yellow design!

8 Complete the text with the correct words.

advertise	design	grown	manufacture
material	option	pick	recycle
sell	throwing		

Online shopping is more popular than ever. Amazon.com has (1) _____ into one of the biggest online marketplaces. There, shoppers can (2) _____ from millions of products of all kinds—clothes, books, shoes, pet food… pretty much every (3) _____ you can imagine!

On the Etsy website, shoppers can find more unique and personal products. Creative, artistic people (4) _____ and (5) _____ their own items, like jewelry, handbags, t-shirts, decorations, and more.

Ebay is another popular site, where people can buy and (6) _____ things. It's a great way for people to (7) _____ items they don't use any more instead of (8) _____ them away. The seller creates a post to (9) _____ the item. The post includes photos and a description of the item, including details such as the size, the (10) _____ it's made out of, and the condition it's in.

9 Extension Choose the correct words to complete the sentences.

1 Department stores have many *displays / bargains* where they show their products for sale, such as jewelry.
2 *Discount / Antique* furniture can be very expensive, especially if it is in good condition and has historical value.
3 Some people don't like online shopping because they don't want to wait for the products to be *delivered / displayed* to their house.
4 If you aren't happy with something you've bought, you can usually take it back to the store and *discount / trade* it for another item.
5 Advertisements are everywhere. They're on TV, on the radio, on the internet, and even on giant *bargains / billboards* for you to see while you're driving.
6 If something is reasonably priced, that means you can *afford / trade* it.

PRONUNCIATION

10 Listen. Underline the stressed word in each compound noun. Then practice saying the words. 🎧 83

1 fishnet
2 plastic bags
3 skateboard
4 recycling program
5 surfboard
6 fishing boat
7 self-esteem
8 electric car

LISTENING

11 Listen to the conversation between two people. You will answer questions about what the speakers say. Choose the correct answer. You will hear the conversation only once. 🎧 84

1 What does the woman ask the man?
   a if he's ever been to Bali
   b if he's seen a certain video
   c If he recycles plastic bags
   d if he has a problem

2 What word does the woman use meaning *to not allow*?
   a prohibit   **c** ban
   b forbid   **d** disallow

3 What is the problem?
   a plastic bags are not made on the island
   b plastic bags get caught in trees
   c plastic bags are more expensive than paper bags
   d plastic bags are not recycled

4 How did the man think about Bali before this conversation?
   a an island with environmental problems
   b an island with great natural beauty
   c an island with way too many tourists
   d an island with a lot of manufacturing

5 What does the Balinese economy depend on?
   a plastic bags   **c** exports
   b tourism   **d** recycling

6 What does the woman think is very inspiring?
   a people who are tough
   b people in beautiful places
   c people in TED Talks
   d people who take action

7 What do the man and woman decide to do?
   a find a way to get more involved in their community
   b find a way to support the Wijsen sisters
   c find a way to start a recycling program in their community
   d find a way to travel to Bali

8 What word does the man use meaning *pride in yourself*?
   a self-respect   **c** self-serving
   b self-worth   **d** self-esteem

A plastic bag floats in the ocean.

12 Listen and answer the questions. 🎧 85

1 What do some people call the Great Pacific Garbage Patch?
   a Waste Island   **c** Trash Island
   b Treasure Island

2 What has brought all the garbage together?
   a ocean currents   **c** fishing nets
   b different countries

3 Where does the trash come from?
   a Texas in the United States
   b North America and Asia
   c a huge garbage patch

4 What is the biggest part of the trash?
   a plastic bottles   **c** plastic bags
   b plastic fishing nets

5 Why is plastic such a problem?
   a it's biodegradable   **c** it's not biodegradable
   b it's recyclable

6 Why does the speaker think countries aren't paying attention to the problem?
   a the problem is far away
   b the problem is too big
   c the problem can't be solved

7 What advice does the speaker give?
   a never, ever use plastic
   b buy reusable materials
   c support "green" companies

GRAMMAR Second conditional

13 Read the sentences. Check the sentences that are second conditional.

1 Stores are designed to make you want to buy things. If shoppers like the music in a store, they are more likely to go in the store and to like its products. ____

2 If the music the store played were slow, people would walk slower—and buy more! ____

3 If you wanted to visit all the stores in the largest shopping mall in the world, you would need many, many hours. ____ It has 1,200 stores!

4 If you work at the West Edmonton Mall, the largest mall in North America, you have 23,000 coworkers. ____ It has 800 stores, a water park, restaurants, and other exciting tourist attractions.

5 If people think online shopping is "greener," they will be wrong. ____ One study showed that the negative effects of transporting goods bought online is greater than people expect.

6 If shopping malls had external windows and clocks, people would be aware of how long they had been there. ____ So designers design malls without them!

7 If you wanted to try on every pair of shoes in Selfridge's in London, you would put on thousands of pairs of shoes. ____ Selfridge's has more than 100,000 pairs of shoes at any time!

14 Match the sentence halves to create sentences with the second conditional.

1 If I found a watch, ____
2 I would not be late all the time ____
3 If I weren't late, ____
4 I would get more job offers ____
5 If I received several job offers, ____
6 If I were able to choose the best job, ____
7 I would be able to buy a watch ____
8 If I bought a watch,

____

a I would earn more money.
b if I earned more money.
c if I had a watch.
d I would return the watch I found!
e I would make a better impression.
f I would know what time it is.
g I would choose the best job.
h if I made a better impression on people.

15 Choose the correct form of the verbs to complete the sentences.

1 He *will bought / would bought / could buy* new clothes if he *save / saved / would save* his money.

2 If our mother *taught / teached / would taught* us how to sew, we *make / could make / made* our own clothes.

3 If the company *not manufactured / did not manufacture / manufactured not* enough smartphones, the price *increased / would increase / would increased*.

4 The stores *are / were / would be* full of unwanted merchandise if no one *buyed / would bought / bought* new clothes.

5 I *would save / saved / would saving* time if I *would shop / shopped / would* closer to my home.

6 If the mall *has / will have / had* better stores, we *would spend probably / would probably spend / spend probably would* more money there.

7 If the bookstore *carries / would carries / carried* more books, I *found / would find / would found* one I like.

8 More people *will eat / ate / would eat* at the restaurant if it *would served / served / serves* better food.

16 Combine the two sentences using the second conditional.

Example: We often buy things we don't really need. We don't have a lot of money in the bank.
If we didn't buy things we don't really need, we would have more money in the bank.

1 Shoppers have so much choice. It can be overwhelming.

____
____

2 We order shoes and sweaters online. They need to be shipped to our homes.

____
____

3 Some people feel better after buying something new. They buy lots of unnecessary things.

____
____

4 Personal shoppers aren't cheap. Very few people are able to hire them.

____
____

5 Stores aim to sell what they think people want. They make a lot of money doing this.

____
____

6 Designers are so creative. They are able to come up with some amazing things.

____
____

8B They want to sell to you

VOCABULARY BUILDING

1 Complete the sentences with the correct words.

air pollution	billboards	sea life	shopping mall
supermarket	TV shows	video games	website

1 There are three _____ about pirates on tonight!

2 This is one of the most difficult _____ I've ever played!

3 Advertisements on _____ are surprisingly effective.

4 A good _____ usually includes a variety of stores.

5 Learning how to build a _____ is a very useful skill.

6 _____ is harmful to people, animals, and plants.

7 Fruits and vegetables are usually displayed at the front of a _____ .

8 Plastics in the ocean are causing great harm to _____ .

READING

2 Write the correct word for each definition. There are two words you don't need.

advertiser	aware	awkward
brand	experiment	product
teenager	TV show	video game
website		

1 a person between the ages of 12 and 20 _____

2 someone who tries to sell things with advertising _____

3 an electronic game with a screen _____

4 knowing about something _____

5 a program you watch _____

6 several internet pages linked together _____

7 something that is made and sold _____

8 not graceful _____

3 Read the following sentences about advertising to teens. Is each sentence correct (C) or incorrect (I)?

1 Teens know exactly what they want. _____

2 Advertisers try to get teens' attention in order to sell things to them. _____

3 Brands take advantage of teens' feelings of insecurity. _____

4 Teens trust advertisers. _____

5 Product placement is only on TV commercials. _____

6 Teens are not influenced by advertising. _____

4 Answer the questions about the article.

1 Advertisers and marketers consider _____ to be an important demographic.
   a peers
   b teens
   c marketers
   d television characters

2 The meaning of the phrase *figuring out* is similar to
   a thinking about.
   b describing problems.
   c trying on clothes.
   d making new friends.

3 According to the article, what about teens do advertisers try to appeal to?
   a their insecurities
   b their budgets
   c their friends
   d their size

4 According to paragraph 2, the following statements are true about teens EXCEPT
   a Many teens feel insecure.
   b Most teens want to fit in with others.
   c Most teens don't want to seem awkward.
   d Most teens want others to be good-looking.

5 The meaning of the word *scenery* is similar to
   a character.
   b background.
   c instrumental music.
   d props.

6 The article agrees with which of these statements?
   a Parents have a big influence on what teens want to buy.
   b Advertisers have a big influence on what teens want to buy.
   c Older teens have a big influence on what younger teens want to buy.
   d TV characters have a big influence on what teens want to buy.

7 Look at the four squares ■ in the article where the following sentence can be added.

They're aware that most teens really want to avoid ever seeming awkward.

Where does the sentence fit?

   a ■ That's because many teenagers are still figuring out what they want to be or to have, so they're willing to experiment with the things they buy.
   b ■ Advertisers and marketers want to get your attention, and convince you that you need a product, so that you'll buy it.
   c ■ They know that teens generally want to fit in, and that they want others to think they are attractive.
   d ■ Think about it the next time you are watching television and a character holds a container of orange juice or a can of soda.

Do you buy it? 🎧 86

1 Do you like to go shopping? Do you shop only for things you need, or do you sometimes shop for things you want but can't afford? Have you ever felt like buying something because you wanted to fit in? If you answered "yes" to any of these questions, then you're just like a lot of other young people! Young people between the ages of 13 and 19 are one of the biggest demographic* groups out there for marketers and advertisers. [■] That's because many teenagers are still figuring out what they want to be or to have, so they're willing to experiment with the things they buy.

2 How do advertisers try to convince you to buy what they're selling? [■] Advertisers and marketers want to get your attention, and convince you that you need a product, so that you'll buy it. Brands* that try to appeal to* teens often use the insecurities many teens feel. [■] They know that teens generally want to fit in, and that they want others to think they are attractive. And because they know that teens are very aware of the importance of peer* groups, advertisers sometimes try to get teenagers to trust their advice on what to have or how to look.

3 What can you do to protect yourself from marketing and advertisements like this? Think about what advertisements are trying to tell you and how they are doing it. If you could buy what they're selling, would it really make you happy? Is the product itself really appealing, or does its appeal come from the models and scenery used to present it? Another thing to look out for is called "product placement." Advertisers and marketers try to show off their products in video games, movies, on television shows, or with websites that are popular with teens. They want young consumers to think, "Oh, those are the shoes that I saw on TV last night!" [■] Think about it the next time you are watching television and a character holds a container of orange juice or a can of soda. Can you see the brand name? That is an example of product placement.

4 Remember, you don't have to let advertisers tell you who you are! Who you are isn't determined by what you buy or own.

demographic *a certain group of people*
brands *goods that are identified by name as the product of a specific manufacturer*
appeal to *to make something desirable to someone*
peer *a person who belongs to the same age group or social group as someone else*

8C New things from old ones

GRAMMAR Defining relative clauses

1 What does the bold word in each sentence refer to?

1 The boy **who** is wearing the striped shirt is my brother.
  a boy
  b me
  c shirt

2 The woman **that** has the sandals and glasses is my aunt.
  a my
  b sandals
  c woman

3 Films **that** have a lot of drama are my favorite.
  a drama
  b films
  c favorite

4 I don't like food **which** is very spicy.
  a me
  b food
  c spicy

5 She likes the flowers **which** have purple and red petals the best.
  a her
  b flowers
  c petals

6 The tree **that** is in our back yard has been there for more than 100 years.
  a back yard
  b 100 years
  c tree

7 People **who** like dogs usually also like cats.
  a cats and dogs
  b like
  c people

2 Complete the sentences with *who, which,* or *that.* There may be more than one correct answer.

1 People _____ live in Buenos Aires call themselves *porteños.*

2 Argentina is a country _____ is famous for tango dancing.

3 A type of coffee _____ is called *cortado* is served in many shops in Buenos Aires.

4 Many shops _____ are in Buenos Aires don't open until 10am.

5 People _____ like sweets might enjoy getting *medialunas*, which are Argentine croissants.

6 Many chefs _____ cook in Buenos Aires' more modern restaurants learned to cook in Europe.

7 Soho and Hollywood are two areas of Buenos Aires _____ have many interesting stores as well as cafes and ice cream shops.

3 Match to complete the sentences.

1 I don't like people _____
2 I like to drink water _____
3 My classmate _____
4 The dog _____
5 My neighbor _____
6 How long has the art _____
7 The painting _____
8 The medicine _____

  a who plays loud music often keeps me up at night.
  b that shows two girls sitting together is beautiful.
  c who are unkind.
  d that Degas painted been at the museum?
  e that he needs is so expensive.
  f who lent me her book said I could keep it until our next class.
  g that isn't filtered.
  h that is barking is disturbing the whole neighborhood.

4 Use the prompts to write sentences with defining relative clauses. Three sentences do not need the relative pronoun.

Example: some people / think / cars / red / faster / other cars
Some people think cars that are red are faster than other cars.
OR
Some people think cars which are red are faster than other cars.

1 the chair / we / bought on sale / so ugly

_____

2 he's / the teacher / gave me / advice / about / my career

_____

3 being / a chemist / the job / I think / I would like / most

_____

4 beans / a food / have / a lot of / nutrition

_____

5 my father / is making / a potato recipe / he found / on the internet

_____

6 the book / is about / man / sailed / around the world / on a small boat

_____

5 Are the words in bold correct? Correct those that are incorrect.

1 I like any **food who has** chocolate in it.

_____

2 Do you want to go to the **restaurants that has** the best chef in town?

_____

3 **People which goes** to my school are the best at science.

_____

4 The **boy who stayed up** all night studying for his science exam was very tired the next day in class.

_____

5 Is being a tour guide a **jobs who pay** a lot of money?

_____

6 Talking to many people every week was very important to the **woman which wanted** to be president.

_____

7 Every **runner who finished** the race received an award.

_____

6 Put the words in the correct order to make sentences.

1 goes / she / Bangkok / has / a / to / brother / who / school / in

_____

2 with / laughed / the / told / woman / everyone / joke / funny / who / the

_____

3 the / that / made / soup / for / was / dinner / delicious / she

_____

4 the / I / see / our / is / girl / new / that / neighbor

_____

5 animal / type / will / an / eat / is / an / that / any / of / omnivore / food

_____

6 they / big / cleaned / tree / that / the / fell down during / the / up / storm

_____

7 not / soda / a / drink / is / is / which / healthy

_____

8 a / uncle / she / an / who / has / is / nurse

_____

7 Complete the paragraph with _which, who,_ and _that_. There may be more than one correct answer.

GoFundMe is a company (1) _____ is based in San Diego, California. Brad Damphousse and Andrew Ballester are the people (2) _____ started the company in 2010. GoFundMe helps people develop websites (3) _____ they can use to raise money for different reasons. People (4) _____ use GoFundMe need money for college, a new business, or have a personal need. Many people visit GoFundMe pages because they want to give money to people (5) _____ need help. And these are pages (6) _____ can really help people! For example, a campaign (7) _____ was trying to help people affected by Hurricane Matthew in 2016 raised $3 million.

8 Use the prompts to write sentences with defining relative clauses that are true for you.

Example: I like apartments _that have balconies_.

1 I like to buy things

_____

2 I like to go to restaurants

_____

3 I like to shop in stores

_____

4 I like to talk to people

_____

5 I visit websites

_____

6 I have classes

_____

7 I know

_____

8 I don't like

_____

8D Our campaign to ban plastic bags in Bali

TEDTALKS

AUTHENTIC LISTENING SKILLS

1 Listen. Complete the sentences. 🎧 87

1 Also, at the _____ Airport of Bali, one of our _____ are planning to start a plastic bag-free policy by 2016.

2 _____ handing out _____ plastic bags and bring in your own _____ bag is our _____ to change that mindset of the public.

3 Our short-term campaign, "One Island / One Voice," is all about this. We _____ and recognize the shops and restaurants that have declared themselves a plastic bag-free zone, and we put _____ at their entrance and publish their names on social media and some important magazines on Bali. And conversely, that highlights those who do _____ the sticker.

WATCH ▶

2 Are the sentences true (T) or false (F)?

1 Almost all plastic bags in Bali end up in rivers or the ocean. _____

2 Melati and Isabel's effort is called "Hello Plastic Bags." _____

3 Their parents took Melati and Isabel to visit the office of Mahatma Ghandhi. _____

4 After the visit, they decided they would stop eating for a cause. _____

5 Melati and Isabel went on a hunger strike without permission from their parents. _____

6 They have been working for almost three years now on their effort. _____

3 Choose the correct words to complete the sentences.

1 Melati and Isabel started a campaign to *help reuse / help reduce* plastic bags in Bali.

2 Their campaign *did well / did not do well*.

3 They learned after their research that there was *something / nothing* good about plastic bags.

4 They went to India to *give a talk / go on a hunger strike*.

5 They convinced their *nutritionist / teachers* to let them go on a hunger strike.

6 They did not eat from *sunrise / noon* until the sun went down every day.

4 Underline the things that Isabel and Melati did and do for their campaign.

1 hunger strike

2 had a business plan

3 social media

4 had a hidden agenda

5 stopped handing out plastic bags

6 remind the governor of his promise

7 check and recognize shops and restaurants that don't have plastic bags

VOCABULARY IN CONTEXT

5 Match the words to the correct paraphrased line from the talk.

1 do something about it _____

2 walk your talk _____

3 go for it _____

4 be the change _____

5 make that difference _____

a **Cause a change.** We're not telling you it's going to be easy.

b So we decided to **take action**.

c Sometimes it does get a little bit hard to **do as you say**.

d So to all the kids of this beautiful but challenging world: **act now**!

e Kids have so much energy and a desire to **live in a way that** the world needs.

6 After everything you have learned about plastic bags, what do you think about their effect on the environment? Are you thinking about making any changes in your life as a result?

8E Call to action

SPEAKING

How to persuade

Use logic:

Research shows that…, Science has proven that…, If…, then…

Use emotion:

Think of…, How would you feel if…, My heart tells me that…

Use morals (right and wrong):

… is the right thing to do, It's wrong to…

1 Complete each sentence with a phrase from the Speaking strategies box. Then decide if the argument is logical (L), emotional (E), or moral (M).

1 _____ smoking causes cancer. ____

2 _____ we should take care of animals. ____

3 _____ recycled more of the plastic we use, _____ less trash would go into the ocean. ____

4 Leaving our children a healthy planet _____. ____

5 _____ there was advertising everywhere you went? ____

6 _____ let people suffer from curable diseases. ____

7 _____ the animals that live in the ocean. They get trapped in the trash and die. ____

8 _____ the Earth is getting warmer. ____

Listen to check your answers. 🎧 **88**

2 Complete the exchanges with the sentences (a–d) and phrases from the Speaking strategy box.

a I don't care. Using renewable energy is the right thing to do.

b Well, how would you feel if they harmed someone in your family?

c Science has proven that animal testing is necessary.

d If we don't use nuclear power, then global warming will increase.

1 **A:** ____
 B: OK, but _____ testing on animals is wrong.

2 **A:** ____
 B: But _____ nuclear energy is more expensive than green energy.

3 **A:** _____ how ugly wind turbines make the countryside look.
 B: ____

4 **A:** _____ put people in prison for life.
 B: ____

3 Think about how you would challenge the views in the sentences below. Make notes and use the speaking strategies. Then listen to sample answers to compare with your ideas. 🎧 **89**

1 The environment is always changing. Global warming is just a myth.

2 There is too much immigration into the country. The government should keep jobs for the local people.

4 You are going to respond to a question. Make notes on your ideas and use the speaking strategies. Speak for 45 seconds and record it. Then listen to a sample answer. 🎧 **90**

Some people shop because they need things and some people shop because they want things. Which do you prefer, and why? Include examples and details in your explanation.

WRITING

1 Read the persuasive blog post. Then label the sections with the correct information.

a adding a call to action
b asking readers to think of an experience
c describing an emotional aspect
d explaining what would be right
e explaining what's wrong
f including a personal story
g introducing the topic
h supplying examples of success
i title

_____ **Community gardens would improve our city**

_____ Some of the best cities in the world have community gardens! These are shared spaces in cities where people work together to grow flowers, vegetables, and fruit. _____ I saw community gardens in Taipei, and in Victoria, Australia. There is also community gardening in Barcelona, London, Seattle, Ottawa, Los Angeles, Honolulu, and many other great cities. Our city has no community gardens, and we believe it should.

_____ Research shows that community gardens bring different people together and help to create an improved sense of community.

_____ Imagine you're walking through a typical urban landscape, all concrete and steel, and suddenly you see the bright colors of a garden right in the city. _____ Wouldn't it make you feel so much better?

_____ Young people in our city center have no access to a real garden. _____ If we allowed community gardens, children would learn more about where food really comes from, plus it would help them to appreciate nature. The gardens would also help to reduce pollution.

_____ Please click here to join our campaign, and get involved today!

---

2 Read the blog post again. Then put the blogger's points in the order they are mentioned 1–7.

_____ community gardens mean less pollution

_____ children learn where food comes from

_____ great cities have community gardens

_____ it helps children to appreciate nature

_____ sense of community is improved

_____ community gardens bring people together

_____ gardens in city centers make us feel better

3 Write a persuasive blog post supporting more independent stores in your town. Listen to the lecture and read the passage. In your blog post, summarize the points made in the the lecture, and be sure to explain how they oppose specific points made in the reading passage. 🎧 **91**

Well-known chain stores continually open new outlets in cities and towns where they have immediate access to large populations. People want products they can trust and, more importantly, they want value for money. From supermarkets to cafes to clothing stores, we all know the familiar brands that deliver on convenience and price. Consumers know where to go for what they need, which chains can supply at low cost and still make a profit.

In principle, everybody wins except, perhaps, independent stores. These typically small stores are generally owned by one or two local people. They cannot possibly compete with the chain stores which are usually run by large corporations. In many cases, they fail after a couple of years and close down. While the idea of independent stores is a nice one, it is not practical. It's simply not realistic for these small stores to provide the same range of products as chain stores, nor to provide goods as cheaply.

Be sure to:

- Introduce your topic with a personal story.
- Mention successful examples of the change you're arguing for.
- Ask readers to think of their own experience and describe the emotional side of your proposal.
- Explain what's wrong and what would be right.
- End with a call to action that explains exactly what you think people should do.

Review

1 Match the related statements.

1 The average American puts 65 pounds of clothing in the trash every year. _____

2 In today's big supermarkets, there are so many brands and varieties of each product, it can be hard to make a decision. _____

3 The toy company Mattel makes around $6 billion dollars per year. _____

4 Shoe manufacturers often use leather, plastic, rubber, cotton, and wood. _____

5 Adidas is producing athletic shoes made from plastic trash picked from the ocean. _____

a There are too many options.
b They throw it away.
c They are recycling.
d They sell a lot of products.
e They use different materials.

2 Complete the sentences with the correct words.

1 Companies a_____ their products so that more people will know about them and buy them.

2 Many electronics, clothes, and other items are m_____ in Chinese factories.

3 It's possible to r_____ objects in creative ways: for example, you can pick a glass bottle out of the trash and make a lamp out of it.

4 Toyota p_____ more than 10 million cars every year.

5 Coco Chanel d_____ simple, stylish clothing for women in Paris in the 1920s.

6 WalMart started as one discount department store in the 1950s and g_____ into one of the largest companies in the world, with more than 11,000 stores in 28 countries.

3 Rearrange the words to complete either the *if*-clause or the main clause (simple past).

1 often / so / buy / they / wouldn't / phones

If people didn't always want the latest and most advanced smartphone,

_____.

2 smartphone / better / them / much / makers / if / pressure / didn't / feel / so / to make

_____,

the manufacturing processes wouldn't need to change.

3 wouldn't / outdated / become / smartphone

If engineers didn't update the hardware and software,

_____.

4 test / if / prototype / the designers / didn't / a

_____

The factory wouldn't be able to make new smartphones

_____.

5 smartphones / be / able / we / new / wouldn't / to buy

_____

if the factory didn't assemble the components.

6 weren't / loaded / if / onto / the software / phone / the

_____,

the phone wouldn't work correctly.

4 Match the sentence halves.

1 If I had enough time to study and clean my apartment, _____

2 If my classes this semester weren't so challenging, _____

3 If I were you, _____

4 If we had a car, _____

5 If I liked vegetables, _____

6 If I had a degree, _____

a I wouldn't take too many classes next semester.
b I could bake a cake for my classmate who is having a birthday next week.
c I could get a good job.
d I would be able to keep up with all the homework that my math teacher assigns.
e I would order the pizza that has tomatoes and onions on it.
f we could go to the park which has the bike trails.

5 Look at the list of words associated with things we buy. Use sentences with defining relative clauses to say what each thing is. Use your dictionary if necessary.

1 plastic bag _____

2 manufacturer _____

3 market _____

4 material _____

5 advertise _____

6 throw away _____

9 All in a Day's Work

9A Work should be fun!

VOCABULARY Jobs

1 Review   Match the words to the definitions.

1 actor ___
2 artist ___
3 receptionist ___
4 farmer ___
5 cook ___
6 waiter/waitress ___
7 businessperson ___
8 photographer ___
9 tour guide ___
10 boss ___
11 driver ___
12 teacher ___

a works at an office; wears a suit; goes to meetings
b shows you around a city or museum
c answers phones; sits at the front desk in an office
d uses a car, truck, taxi, or bus to do his/her job
e serves food at a restaurant
f helps people learn
g manages and supervises people
h works on-screen in movies or television
i takes pictures with a camera
j makes food; works in the kitchen
k grows food; often in a rural area
l creates beautiful or interesting objects to look at

2 Review   Choose the correct words to complete the sentences.

1 Frida Kahlo, Michelangelo, and Pablo Picasso are all famous *actors / artists*.
2 When you are done with your meal in a restaurant, ask the *waiter / teacher* for the bill.
3 Before you can enter a large office building, you usually have to check in with the *boss / receptionist* and show your ID.
4 Museums are always interesting, but you can learn more if you pay a *driver / guide* to take you around and explain the items.
5 Many towns have weekend markets where you can buy vegetables and other products from local *farmers / photographers*.
6 In the downtown area at lunchtime, you can see many *businesspeople / receptionists* from local offices on their cell phones or having lunch meetings. They never seem to stop working!
7 Often, people who work as *cooks / bosses* don't want to make their own meals at home.

3 Match the words to the definitions.

1 cleaner ___
2 accountant ___
3 lawyer ___
4 factory worker ___
5 construction worker ___
6 salesperson ___
7 paramedic ___
8 nurse ___

a a person who builds houses
b a person who washes the floors, vacuums, takes out trash, etc.
c a person who works at a hospital and helps sick and injured people
d a person who drives an ambulance and responds to medical emergencies
e an office worker who is very good with numbers
f a person who makes money when people buy their products
g a person who helps to put together, pack, and ship products
h a high-paid worker who represents other people who are victims of crimes or who are accused of crimes

4 Listen. What is each person's job? Choose the correct answer. 🎧 92

1 a lawyer
  b high school teacher
  c police officer

2 a firefighter
  b construction worker
  c nurse

3 a accountant
  b doctor
  c chief executive

4 a electrical engineer
  b software engineer
  c salesperson

5 a office worker
  b construction worker
  c architect

6 a chef
  b manager
  c chief executive

5 Complete the text. Write one word in each space.

If you're thinking about pursuing a high-paying career, you should consider going to college, and maybe even graduate school. A (1) _____ usually spends four years at college then three years at law school. A (2) _____ needs even more: four years in college, then four years of medical school and three to four years of residency training. If the business world is more your style, then you'll need a four-year business degree plus a master's degree (MBA) in order to become the (3) _____ of a company.

But if a four-year university isn't your thing, you can still become successful. For example, if you're a people person, and you're good at selling, you could become a well-paid (4) _____. You could be hired by a big company! Or, you could attend cooking school and become a (5) _____. You might work at a great restaurant, or even start your own restaurant. Maybe you could even be a celebrity chef on TV!

A lot of people start out as a low-paid worker and move up in the company, becoming a (6) _____ responsible for other people. For example, you could spend a few years working in carpentry as a (7) _____, gain building skills and knowledge, and eventually become the boss or start your own building company. It's the same in other industries. You could start out as a (8) _____ and one day open your own cleaning company.

Whatever you choose, put your heart into it, and you will achieve success!

6 **Extension** Read the letter that follows. A word or phrase is missing in some of the sentences. Four answer choices are given below each of the sentences. Select the correct words to complete the text.

Dear Ms. O'Connell:
I'm writing in response to the accounting job you posted yesterday. I am currently (1) _____ as an accountant at a small company, and I enjoy working here.

   a getting a job   **c** unemployed
   b out of work   **d** employed

However, this was my first job after graduating college, and I have been here for six years. So now I am ready for a new (2) _____.

   a internship   **c** challenge
   b freedom   **d** excitement

In a small company, there is not a lot of room to grow. For this reason, I am interested in the (3) _____ to work in a large and growing company such as yours.

   a opportunity   **c** employment
   b excitement   **d** benefit

I think the experience will really help my (4) _____.

   a adventure   **c** salary
   b career   **d** application

I have attached my (5) _____ for your review. There, you can see the details of my work experience.

   a salary   **c** apply
   b employment   **d** resume

You will see that I am (6) _____ of four large accounts, and I also manage the interns.

   a full-time   **c** out of work
   b in charge   **d** an expert

I think you'll find that I am a quick learner and (7) _____ who will always do the best job I possibly can. I am sure my boss would agree.

   a an assistant   **c** a hard worker
   b professional   **d** slow

I would like to meet with you as soon as possible to discuss the job further and to learn more about the salary and (8) _____.

   a benefits   **c** danger
   b adventure   **d** assistants

Please feel free to call or email. I look forward to speaking with you.

Sincerely,
Sheldon Harlow, CPA

PRONUNCIATION

7 Listen. Does the intonation rise or fall at the end of each question? Then practice saying the questions. 🎧 **93**

1 rising ∧   falling ∨   **5** rising ∧   falling ∨
2 rising ∧   falling ∨   **6** rising ∧   falling ∨
3 rising ∧   falling ∨   **7** rising ∧   falling ∨
4 rising ∧   falling ∨   **8** rising ∧   falling ∨

LISTENING

8 Listen to the speakers and choose their jobs. 🎧 **94**

1 **a** fisherman
  b veterinarian
  c marine biologist

2 **a** paramedic
  b doctor
  c mechanic

3 **a** lawyer
  b architect
  c teacher

4 **a** paramedic
  b factory worker
  c software engineer

5 **a** architect
  b accountant
  c teacher

6 **a** chef
  b farmer
  c grocer

9 Listen to the conversation and answer the questions. 🎧 **95**

1 What had the young man already done by the time he was in high school?
  a decided to become a nurse
  b taken online classes
  c worked a few jobs

2 What position is the man applying for?
  a nurse
  b orderly
  c gurney

3 Why does this man think that this job is different from his previous ones?
  a He thinks it's a serious job.
  b He thinks it pays more money.
  c He thinks it will be a lot of fun.

4 What do orderlies do?
  a clean patients   **c** move patients
  b feed patients

5 What word means *a kind of bed on wheels*?
  a a gurney   **c** a transport
  b a wheelchair

6 What does the man eventually want to become?
  a an orderly   **c** a doctor
  b a registered nurse

7 When the woman says "stranger things have happened," what does she mean?
  a that she wouldn't be very surprised
  b that she thinks it's very unusual
  c that she really doesn't expect it to happen

10 Listen and answer the questions. 🎧 **96**

1 What would be the best title for this talk?
  a Overworked and underpaid
  b Live to work or work to live?
  c Life is work and work is life
  d How to retire early

2 What does the speaker ask questions about?
  a the balance between working days and nights
  b the balance between work and life
  c the best ways to find happiness
  d the negative impact of life on work

3 Why do some people say it's OK to work as long and as hard as necessary?
  a because life is very expensive
  b because you have to earn success
  c because you shouldn't waste time
  d because a personal life isn't important

4 How would you describe a person who works 60 hours a week?
  a very lazy
  b very angry
  c very busy
  d very wealthy

5 What do you think the expression *around the clock* means?
  a working a 12-hour day
  b from noon to midnight
  c after work
  d all day and all night

6 Which point of view does the speaker agree with?
  a the first one
  b the second one
  c neither one
  d both

GRAMMAR Past perfect

11 Identify the tense of the underlined verb in each sentence. Is the sentence simple past (S), present perfect (P), or past perfect (PP).

1 By the time I <u>had found</u> a job, I didn't have any money left. _____

2 I <u>did not go</u> to college after school; I took a gap year. _____

3 My friend <u>has had</u> a job at a bookstore since last summer. _____

4 The job market <u>had</u> already <u>become</u> worse when I returned from traveling. _____

5 My girlfriend <u>stayed</u> here and helped her grandparents after she graduated. _____

6 <u>Have</u> you <u>worked</u> in a skyscraper downtown for a long time? _____

7 The company <u>had advertised</u> my job online. _____

8 My cousins and I <u>went</u> to the beach every day last summer. _____

12 Read the sentences. Which action happened first (1), and which happened second (2)?

1 Before she went to college, she had gone to school in her town.
go to college: _____
go to school: _____

2 I put on clean clothes after I had taken a shower.
put on clothes: _____
take shower: _____

3 Before he planted the seeds, we had prepared the soil.
plant seeds: _____
prepare soil: _____

4 They had tried very hard, but they lost the game by one point.
try hard: _____
lose game: _____

5 Before they saw the movie, they had read the book.
see movie: _____
read book: _____

6 After she had read the online job posting, she updated her resume.
read job posting: _____
update resume: _____

7 He enjoyed his job after his manager had promoted him.
enjoy job: _____
get promotion: _____

8 She fixed the software bug after she had identified the error in the code.
fix software bug: _____
identify error: _____

13 Listen to the job interview. Then complete the sentences. 🎧 **97**

1 What had Martina done at home?
She _____ her parents cook meals at home.

2 What had Martina learned at school?
She _____ the basics of working in a restaurant kitchen as well as the usual high school subjects.

3 What had Martina done at her aunt's restaurant?
She _____ the tables and _____ food to the guests.

4 What had Martina done at the Greek restaurant?
She _____ a cook and _____ the main dishes.

5 What had Martina done as chef at the Japanese restaurant?
As chef, she _____ the menus and _____ the food.

14 Correct the errors with the past perfect in the sentences.

1 Before you text your friend, had you receive your teacher's email?

_____

2 After the teacher had give them the assignment, they go to the library to research the topic.

_____

3 Before you had ate dinner, you had finish your homework.

_____

4 After the meeting, the manager prepare a schedule that work for everyone.

_____

5 Before we had cooked lunch, we had buy all the ingredients.

_____

6 He creates a fan website for his favorite band after he had saw a fan site for another band.

_____

7 Had you meet before I had introduce you yesterday?

_____

9B Green science

VOCABULARY BUILDING

1 Match the sentence halves.

1 Scientists and engineers ___
2 Ideas taken from computer science and chemistry ___
3 Zaro Bates grows food on an urban farm ___
4 One important source of green energy ___
5 Wind energy and clean cars ___

a are often used in clean car technology.
b work together on the development of clean cars.
c borrows power from ocean waves.
d are two types of exciting, green technology.
e and sells it at a community food stand.

READING

2 Answer the questions about the article.

1 The author uses the phrase *play a big role* in paragraph 1 to mean
   a be a source of green energy.
   b be on stage.
   c be important.
   d be worth a lot of money.

2 The word *green* in paragraph 1 means
   a not natural.
   b not harmful to the environment.
   c relating to the wind and ocean.
   d natural.

3 What is the author's purpose?
   a to help people find jobs
   b to help sell electric cars
   c to give examples of green jobs
   d to give an opinion on the best jobs

4 The author's description of the urban farm does not include which of the following details?
   a The farm produces honey.
   b There are chickens at the farm.
   c Some of the food goes to food banks.
   d The farm produces a lot of food.

5 The meaning of the word *generate* in paragraph 5 is similar to
   a produce.   **c** power.
   b reduce.   **d** turn on.

6 According to paragraph 5, what does a wave farm produce?
   a electricity   **d** clean fuel
   b wind
   c technology

3 Match the job with the description.

1 urban farmer ___
2 software developer ___
3 production manager ___
4 chemical engineer ___
5 materials scientist ___

a studies materials and how to use them
b plans the activities needed to manufacture something
c works on making batteries better
d grows enough food to sell in a city
e works with the computer in the car

4 Complete the sentences with the correct words.

1 Chemical and electrical ___ work together to develop clean car technology.
   a vehicles
   b engineers
   c manufacture
   d managers

2 Software developers use ideas ___ computer science to create computers for clean cars.
   a belong to
   b made from
   c taken from
   d added to

3 Wave energy will be an important source of ___ energy in the future.
   a solar
   b renewable
   c power
   d technology

4 Clean cars, urban farms, and wave energy are three types of ___ jobs that we can look forward to in the future.
   a green
   b engineering
   c electrical
   d renewable

5 Answer the questions about the article with your own ideas.

1 What kind of green work would you like to know more about?
   _____
   _____

2 Do you know anyone who works in a green job? What does he or she do?
   _____
   _____

3 Do you think green jobs are important? Why or why not?
   _____
   _____

Green Jobs of the Future ⌂ 98

1 You've heard about green energy, green buildings, and green products. The future is green, and green jobs will play a big role in that future. Is there a green job in your future? Have you thought about what you'd like to do when you're ready to start working? If you have, then you might want to learn more about green jobs like these.

Clean Cars

2 People with different skills work on developing electric, or clean, vehicles from the first designs to manufacturing a car. These projects require people with backgrounds in science, engineering, math, computers, business, and manufacturing.

- Chemical engineers bring ideas from chemistry and use them to design or improve equipment. An important part of their work is developing and improving battery designs.

- Materials scientists study what materials, such as aluminum, are being used in electric cars and their batteries. They examine what materials are made of in order to improve them or create new ones. For example, electric cars need to be lightweight, so a materials scientist needs to identify strong and lightweight materials to use.

- Electrical engineers design, develop, and test the electrical parts of the vehicle. They design the system that makes it possible for a gas engine and a battery to work together.

- Software developers use their knowledge of math and computers to design software that controls the car engine. Electric and hybrid cars have built-in computers that control the engine and battery systems depending on the situation.

- Production managers plan and organize the people, equipment, and parts needed to build and assemble vehicles and vehicle parts.

Urban Farming

3 Zaro Bates runs a farm on Staten Island in New York City. The farm is between two large apartment buildings, but it's not a garden. At 4,500 square feet (465 square meters), it is a commercial farm that produces vegetables and other products for sale. In fact, one day a week from the spring to the fall Zaro sells produce at the apartments.

4 What does Bates grow on the urban farm? About 50 different kinds of produce* including vegetables and herbs. The farm even produces honey. In fact, Bates is able to grow so much food that she donates some of it to food banks.

Wave Energy

5 Ocean waves are a powerful source of renewable energy. Wave energy is green, and it can be used in ways that do not harm sea life. A wave power "farm" is a number of machines that generate electricity from power created by the waves. One type of wave power farm operates on the energy that's created when a float on a large buoy* moves with the waves in the ocean. The Aguçadoura Wave Farm, the world's first, is off the coast of northern Portugal.

6 Wave energy is a new technology, but it holds great promise. Engineers, managers, and scientists will be the wave "farmers" of the future. Could there be a wave in your future?

produce *vegetables, fruit, herbs*
buoy *a floating object used to mark something underwater*

9C He said he studied for the exam

GRAMMAR Reported speech

1 Listen and complete the sentences. 🎧 99

1 She told her sons it _____ time for dinner.

2 Lee _____ if I had been to Cambodia.

3 I told Lee _____ to Cambodia when I was in high school.

4 She _____ *Harry Potter and the Philosopher's Stone* was her favorite book.

5 Sofie _____ Buenos Aires was her favorite city.

6 Kanata said _____ to the Sydney Opera House.

7 He _____ he was worried he would fail the exam because he forgot to study.

8 My father _____ if I wanted some bread with my soup.

2 Choose the correct reported speech option for each direct speech.

1 My grandmother: "Always work smarter, not harder."
  a My grandmother said to always work smarter, not harder.
  b My grandmother will say to always work smarter, not harder.

2 Martin: "I studied all week for the exam and know I will get a good score."
  a Martin said he could be studying all week for the exam and knows he'd get a good score.
  b Martin said he'd studied all week for the exam and knew he'd get a good score.

3 My grandfather: "You've made me proud."
  a My grandfather told me I had made him proud.
  b My grandfather told me I had him proud.

4 Me: "Is Jane Goodall an important scientist?"
  a I ask if Jane Goodall is an important scientist.
  b I asked if Jane Goodall was an important scientist.

5 My sister: "I rode my bike to school every day last year."
  a My sister said me she rode her bike to school every day last year.
  b My sister told me she rode her bike to school every day last year.

6 My uncle: "The train won't be on time."
  a My uncle said the train wouldn't be on time.
  b My uncle said be the train can't be on time.

7 My friends Carlos and Luis: "We can't come to your party this weekend."
  a Carlos and Luis said they couldn't come to my party this weekend.
  b Carlos and Luis said they could come to my party this weekend.

8 Eun: "I can look after your pets while you're on vacation."
  a Eun told me she could look after my pets while I'm on vacation.
  b Eun told me she will look after my pets while I was on vacation.

3 Choose the correct words to complete the sentences.

1 The salesman said, "You will have to pay more money for the car you want."
  He said that I *would / could* have to pay more money for the car I wanted.

2 She said, "I'm traveling to Chile for work."
  She *told that / told me that* she *was traveling / traveled* to Chile for work.

3 "I visited my grandmother every week," she told her friend.
  She / You told her friend that she *had visited / wouldn't visit* her grandmother every week.

4 My friend asked, "Do you want to go cycling tomorrow?"
  He asked if I wanted to go cycling *the next day / tomorrow*.

5 He asked, "What are you writing?"
  He *said / asked* me what I *was writing / had written*.

6 Dad said, "Mei, open our windows to let some cooler air in."
  Dad *told Mei to / told to Mei* open *our / their* windows to let some cooler air in.

7 Sejal said, "I've gone to Majorca for vacation."
  Sejal told me *she'd gone / she went* to Majorca for vacation.

8 I said, "Sejal, I went to Majorca last year."
  I told Sejal I *had gone / had been going to* Majorca last year.

4 Put the words in the correct order.

1 couldn't / he / them / eat / told / the / salad / they

_____

2 was / he / some / he / going / to / said / eggs / buy

_____

3 that / late / she / she / could / tell / our / I'd / be / for / said / class / teacher

_____

4 he / travel / planning / told / he's / me / to / to / Asia

_____

5 worked / they / me / project / told / they / on / that

_____

6 she / the / she / previous / watched / the / news / said / night

_____

7 couldn't / parents / they / eat / dinner / with / they / their / said

_____

8 asked / would / he / him / if / help / I

_____

5 Put the words in the correct categories to show tense changes from direct speech to reported speech. Use one word twice.

past perfect	present continuous	simple past
simple past	will / won't	

Direct speech	Reported speech
simple present	
	past continuous
	simple past / past perfect
present perfect	
	would / wouldn't

6 Are the words in bold correct? Correct those that are incorrect.

1 He **told he** couldn't lend me any money.

_____

2 She **asked me** not to go to the beach without her.

_____

3 He said one of the best art museums in the country **was** in our city.

_____

4 Marta said **she'd** look it up online.

_____

7 Listen to the radio report. Then rewrite the sentences as reported speech. 🎧 **100**

1 The reporter said, "It's 10pm on a cool Saturday in Los Angeles."

_____

2 The reporter said, "The truck will be open for another several hours…"

_____

3 The reporter said, "Kogi BBQ has been popular since 2008…"

_____

4 The reporter said, "…two friends had an idea to serve Korean barbecue together with Mexican tacos…"

_____

8 Choose the correct words to complete the sentences.

1 She told me she _gave / given_ people legal advice and information. She's a _lawyer / nurse_.

2 He said he _was trained / won't trained_ to help people who are sick or injured, and he received more training than a nurse. He's a _chef / doctor_.

3 She said she _that was helping / was going to help_ teenagers learn. She will be a _high school teacher / dentist_.

4 They _told us / told_ they designed devices like music players and smartphones. They're _accountants / software engineers_.

5 He said he _can / couldn't_ provide care for people's teeth and mouth. He's not a _dentist / teacher_.

6 She told us she _designed / will design_ computer programs and software. She's an _architect / electronics engineer_.

7 He told me he _won't / could_ prepare financial information. He's an _architect / accountant_.

8 They said they _prepared and cooked / going to prepare and cook_ food as a job. They're _chefs / lawyers_.

9 Rewrite the sentences as reported speech.

1 Jian said, "I can't print my paper from that computer."

_____

2 She said, "I lived in Copenhagen until I was in high school."

_____

3 She said, "Yesterday I walked from our school to the library."

_____

4 My parents said, "We turned the lights on."

_____

5 He said, "I can't take the history exam today."

_____

6 My sister said, "I'm looking for extra math exercises online."

_____

9D The surprising thing I learned sailing solo around the world

TEDTALKS

AUTHENTIC LISTENING SKILLS

1 Listen. Circle the weak forms in the sentences with the schwa sound. 🔊 **101**

I will never forget the excitement as we closed the coast. I will never forget the feeling of adventure as I climbed on board the boat and stared into her tiny cabin for the first time. But the most amazing feeling was the feeling of freedom, the feeling that I felt when we hoisted her sails.

WATCH ▶

2 Order the events (1–6) from the talk.

___ She begins her apprenticeship in sailing.

___ She sits in a design meeting designing a boat for her to travel alone around the world.

___ Dame Ellen MacArthur sails for the first time.

___ She misses an iceberg by 20 feet.

___ She finishes in second place.

___ She saves her school dinner money change for eight years.

3 Are the sentences true (T) or false (F)?

1 When Ellen was a child, she often dreamed of sailing. ___

2 During a race, her boat blew to its side in the Southern Ocean. ___

3 She was at sea for three years for the race. ___

4 She enjoyed the race so much, she decided to do another race and sail around the world. ___

5 She says that a boat is an entire world and what you take is all you have. ___

6 Sailing on a boat helped Ellen to understand that there is an end to things—what we have is all we have. ___

4 Choose the correct answers.

1 What is the speaker mainly discussing?
a how sailing is the best hobby
b how she went from sailing to what she does now
c why coal is limited and important

2 What does the speaker do now?
a She runs an organization.
b She sails in races.
c She speaks about sailing.

3 Why does the speaker mention the photo of a coal-fired power station?
a to describe how coal is an important part of energy
b to talk about the coal industry
c to connect the photo to her great-grandfather

4 What does the speaker want to do with the things people use?
a She wants to use up materials.
b She wants to think of ways to reuse things.
c She wants to collect the things people use.

5 What can be inferred about the Ellen MacArthur Foundation?
a It helps build an economy that can help the future.
b It helps young people live their dream of sailing.
c It helps old people understand technology.

6 Why does the speaker mention her great-grandfather?
a to explain how old he is
b to explain how there were only 25 cars during his time
c to explain how much the world has changed

VOCABULARY IN CONTEXT

5 Match the words to the correct paraphrased line from the talk.

1 focus on ___
2 global ___
3 use up ___
4 freedom ___
5 tough ___
6 curiosity ___

a The most amazing feeling was the feeling of having **the right to do what I want**.

b Just like in my dreams, there were amazing parts and **difficult** parts.

c Our **world** economy is no different.

d And it made me make a decision that I never thought I would make: to leave solo sailing to **look closely at** the great challenge I'd ever seen.

e And my **desire to know more** led me to some extraordinary places.

f If we could build an economy that would use things rather than **take all of something,** we could make a future that works in the long term.

9E What do you do?

SPEAKING

1 Put the words in the correct order.

1 nurses / do / much / earn / how

_____?

2 do / what / consultant / an / does / image

_____?

3 been / architecture / I've / in / interested / always

_____.

4 gamers / do / work / where / professional

_____?

5 paid / teachers / are / well

_____?

6 one / history / subjects / of / favorite / is / my

_____.

7 need / what / skills / do / salespeople

_____?

2 Look at the questions below and decide if the intonation rises (R) or falls (F) at the end of the sentence. Then listen and check your answers. 🎧 102

1 Do you work every day? ___
2 Have you ever had a part-time job? ___
3 How many hours do nurses work? ___
4 Which company do you work for? ___
5 How much training do professional gamers have? ___
6 What qualifications do teachers need? ___
7 Would you like to be a firefighter? ___
8 Are you going to get promoted? ___

3 Match the sentence halves.

1 What does an online reputation manager ___
2 So, where do online reputation managers ___
3 I ___
4 I love ___
5 So, what skills do these managers ___

a work?
b like singing.
c need?
d social media.
e do?

4 Complete the conversation with the sentences from Activity 3.

A: Everyone's talking about careers, but I don't know what I want to do when I'm older.
B: I know, my Dad said I needed to make some decisions, but (1) _____ and he doesn't think that's a career.
A: So, what have you said to him?
B: Well, (2) _____, and there's more work in that field. One new job that sounds interesting is called an online reputation manager.
A: I've never heard of that before! (3) _____
B: Well, they deal with complaints and problems on social media before they become big issues.
A: OK, wait a minute. (4) _____
B: Usually for big companies, but it could be for bands and singers too. That's what I'd be interested in doing.
A: That sounds cool! (5) _____
B: Well, online complaints can cause companies huge problems, so you have to be quick to respond to things, and have great people skills, and be able to communicate clearly on social media, which is great for me.
A: I might have to think about a new job too. I love IT; maybe I should look at designing social media apps or something.
B: Yeah, go for it. I think there's a job out there for everyone.

5 Read the question and make some notes on your ideas for your response. Speak for two minutes and record your answer. Then, listen to the sample answer. 🎧 103

What kind of job would you like to have in the future?

WRITING Indirect questions

1 Read the email. Answer the questions with the correct words or phrases. Two items are not used.

a journalist	a travel writer	Alvaro Costa	formal
Ms. Dixon	no	Piero Costa	yes

Dear Ms. Dixon,

My uncle, Piero Costa, gave me your name and said that you can answer some of my questions about travel writing. Thank you for taking the time to read my email. I'm in grade 11 at the Heaton High School in Toronto. I'm very interested in both travel and writing, and I would like to learn more about becoming a travel writer.

I have a few questions:

1 I'm not sure what subjects to major in. Could you tell me whether it's better to take journalism or English at college?

2 I have already written some travel writing articles, but I don't know where to send them. Do you know if there's a magazine or website that might publish them?

3 I'm trying to read as much travel writing as I can. I'd like to know who your favorite travel writers are.

Thank you again for agreeing to answer my questions. I look forward to hearing from you.

Yours sincerely,
Alvaro Costa

---

1 Who has information about travel writing?

_____

2 Who is a student?

_____

3 What does Alvaro want to become?

_____

4 Has Alvaro written any travel writing pieces?

_____

5 Does he say who his favorite travel writers are?

_____

6 What is the tone of the email?

_____

2 Choose the best option to complete the formal email.

Dear Mr. Miller,

My teacher, Mr. Benevides, has given me your name. He said that you can answer some of my questions about web design. (1) ___ I'm in my final year at the Oakvale High School in Singapore. I'm very interested in web design and development, and (2) ___

I have some questions for you.

1 (3) ___ Could you tell me about an average day in your job? Do you have to go to a lot of meetings?

2 I already help some of my family members with their websites, and I think I could start my own business. (4) ___

3 I'd like to take some online courses on coding. (5) ___

Many thanks for taking the time to answer my questions. (6) ___

Yours sincerely,
Junsu Chang

---

1 a Thank you so much for this opportunity.
  b I don't know any web developers, so thanks.

2 a I really want you to tell me about being a web developer.
  b I would like to learn more about being a web developer.

3 a I'd like to know what a typical day is like for a web developer.
  b Anyway, what's a typical day like for most web developers?

4 a So, is it better to work for a big company or to become self-employed?
  b Do you know if it's better to work for a big company or to be self-employed?

5 a Could you tell me which courses you recommend?
  b What courses do you recommend in coding?

6 a Please write back soon, Mr. Miller!
  b I look forward to hearing from you.

3 Now write a formal email of your own. Choose one of the careers, and follow the steps.

Choose one career:

- police officer
- advertising executive
- make-up artist
- marketing assistant

1 Use polite and formal language.
2 Address your email to Mr. Noguchi.
3 Say you got his name from your teacher, Ms. Powell.
4 Thank him for the opportunity.
5 Give him some information about yourself.
6 Ask him at least three indirect questions.
7 Thank him again and request a reply.
8 Sign off appropriately.

Review

1 Choose the correct words to complete the sentences.

1 To apply for a job as a salesperson, you should talk to the *store manager / chef*.

2 The *lawyers / paramedics* are usually called when there is a medical emergency.

3 After a big office party, the building *cleaners / architects* may have a lot of extra work to do.

4 In order to become a *dentist / factory worker*, you must complete several years of college.

5 *Office workers / Firefighters* have a difficult and dangerous job protecting people and their homes and businesses, as well as our forests.

6 In order to become an *accountant / executive*, you need to be good at math and keeping records.

2 Complete the sentences with the correct words.

1 One thing an e_____ e_____ might do is design and test the computer-based parts of a car.

2 The c_____ e_____ is the most senior and usually the highest-paid person in a company.

3 A p_____ o_____ has a very important job protecting the community from crime.

4 We pay a lot of money for our computers, cell phones, and designer clothes, but the f_____ w_____ who make them often don't earn very much money at all.

5 At the hospital, we depend on d_____ to explain our condition and give us advice, but it's the n_____ who take care of us.

6 You always know when f_____ are on the way because of the loud sirens and bright flashing lights on their long, red trucks.

3 Look at the dates and events in Sheryl Sandberg's life. Complete the sentences about her using the past perfect form of the verbs.

1969	born in Washington, DC
1991	BA in economics from Harvard
1992	Research Assistant at the World Bank
1995	MBA from Harvard Business School
1996	Chief of Staff at U.S. Department of Treasury
2001	a vice president at Google
2008	Chief Operating Officer at Facebook
2012	became first woman on Facebook's Board of Directors

| be | complete | earn |
| graduate | work (x2) | |

Sheryl Sandberg is the chief operating officer at Facebook.

1 She attended Harvard University after she _____ from high school.

2 She worked at the World Bank after she _____ her studies at Harvard.

3 She went back to Harvard for her MBA after she _____ at the World Bank.

4 Before she worked at the U.S. Department of Treasury, she _____ her MBA.

5 She _____ a vice president at Google for seven years before she got her current job at Facebook.

6 She became the first woman on the Facebook board of directors after she _____ as chief operating officer of Facebook for four years.

4 Complete the sentences using the past simple or past perfect form of the verbs in parentheses.

1 He told me he _____ (enjoy; past perfect) that internship at the museum.

2 She said that in ancient Japan, farmers _____ rice and _____ (grow, sell; past simple) it.

3 Kwan told me he _____ (find; past perfect) some good places to eat near his hotel.

4 She told me she _____ (eat; past simple) lunch with her coworkers before the meeting.

5 He said he _____ (want; past simple) to find a new job.

6 She said she _____ (decide; past perfect) to study English.

5 Read each question. Choose the correct answer.

1 Do you think he'll be a great dancer?
a Well, his teachers told him that if he practiced more, he could be a great dancer.
b Yes! His teachers are telling him that if he'd practiced more, he would be a great dancer.

2 Is your teacher famous?
a Yes, he told that he's on a winning Olympic soccer team in the 1990s.
b Yes, he said that he'd been on a winning Olympic soccer team in the 1990s.

3 Did you win the award?
a No, my principal told me I didn't win it.
b Yes! My principal had told me I was winning it.

4 Do you know where Maria and Pedro lived when they were children?
a They told me they could live in Bogota when they were children.
b Their mother said they'd lived in Bogota until they were teenagers.

10 Remote Control

10A Inventions: past, present, future

VOCABULARY Technology

1 Review Complete the sentences with the correct words.

camera	machine	printer	program
software	texts	tablet	video games

1 A computer is a _____ that performs many functions, including word processing, counting, and storing information.

2 A _____ is like a computer, but it's smaller and has a keyboard on the screen.

3 Most cell phones have a pretty good _____ for taking and posting photos.

4 For many people, playing _____ is a fun and challenging activity that uses several skills.

5 If you don't have access to a _____, you can send your essay to your teacher in an email.

6 I don't like talking on the phone. I usually communicate by sending _____.

7 If you know how to _____ computers, you could create _____ for a big company like Apple or Microsoft.

2 Match the words and the definitions.

1 research ____	**a** an object that helps you do a job
2 equipment ____	**b** all of the things that are used to do something
3 process ____	**c** improvement that is made over time
4 tool ____	**d** steps that you take to do something
5 invention ____	**e** to make something or someone do what you want
6 progress ____	**f** to find out information about something
7 control ____	**g** a new object that someone creates

3 Choose the correct words to complete the sentences.

1 You need a lot of ____ to go camping, such as a flashlight, a tent, and food.
   a inventions   **b** equipment   **c** process

2 Today we have powerful electric machines to do our work for us, but more than a thousand years ago, people were constructing houses and huge buildings of stone using only very simple ____.
   a research   **b** tools   **c** developments

3 These days, almost everything is digital. Instead of going to a store to buy a CD, getting new music is now a simple ____ of going to a website or app and downloading files.
   a technology   **b** progress   **c** process

4 Did you know that there are some new video games that you can ____ with your brain by wearing a special device on your head?
   a control   **b** research   **c** process

5 Several companies are working on the ____ of the flying car. Some have succeeded, but it will be years before many people will be able to buy and use them.
   a equipment   **b** progress   **c** development

6 The many important ____ that were developed during the Industrial Revolution, such as the steam engine and the locomotive train, quickly and dramatically changed Europe's cities.
   a technology   **b** inventions   **c** developments

4 Read the text about tiny robots. Are the sentences right, wrong, or does the text not say?

TINY ROBOTS

Since the invention of the first digital and programmable robot in 1954, robot technology has made incredible progress. Robots are now used in many different places, including factories, hospitals, and the military. Robotic equipment is used for underwater research and space exploration. Robots are sent into buildings and other places that are too dangerous for people to enter.

When we think of robots, we often think of large machines—sometimes we imagine human-like machines that have a face and talk. But an interesting new development is the field of micro- and nano-robotics.

Across the globe, scientists are making and testing very tiny robots. They hope these robots will be able to go into the human body and perform tasks, such as delivering medicine to a specific area, removing a small object that was swallowed, performing surgery, or making tiny repairs. They are controlled wirelessly and remotely from outside the body, but scientists hope one day to create robots that can be programmed to work independently, or through a process of working together with other tiny robots.

Some people fear having their jobs replaced by robots, but robots could actually save their lives one day. Tiny robots could become one of the most important tools in the hospitals of the future!

1 Robots have replaced around 40% of human jobs since the 1950s.
   a right   **b** wrong   **c** doesn't say

2 Robots are used to explore the oceans and outer space.
   a right   **b** wrong   **c** doesn't say

3 Very tiny robots are a standard part of most hospitals' equipment today.
   a right   **b** wrong   **c** doesn't say

4 Scientists use a kind of remote control to move the robots inside the patient's body.
   a right   **b** wrong   **c** doesn't say

5 Micro- and nano-robots will be an important tool for doctors to use in the future.
   a right   **b** wrong   **c** doesn't say

6 Robots can do many jobs people can't do.
   a right   **b** wrong   **c** doesn't say

7 The first micro-robot was invented in 1954.
   a right   **b** wrong   **c** doesn't say

8 A lab in Japan is testing micro-robot technology to help people with stomach problems.
   a right   **b** wrong   **c** doesn't say

⑤ Extension Choose the correct words to complete the sentences.

1 After you download the software, you need to *install / produce* it on your computer.

2 The *energy / electric* that powers a cell phone comes from a battery.

3 Scientists send robots to *engineer / explore* extremely deep areas of the ocean in hopes that they will *install / discover* something new and interesting.

4 In the future, I hope we can use *green technology / spacecraft* to reduce pollution.

5 The Swedish tech company King *produces / partners with* many popular game apps for computers and phones.

6 Some robots have been *discovered / engineered* to work independently, without a person there to control them.

7 Some cell phone companies *partner with / explore* specific service providers to offer special deals.

⑥ Extension Complete the texts with the correct words.

design	discovered	electric	energy
engineer	explore	green technology	install
invention	partnering with	producing	spacecraft

1 3D printers are a useful _____. People can _____ a 3-D digital model of an object and then "print" it using materials like plastic, creating a solid object.

2 Cassini-Huygens is a robotic _____ that NASA sent to _____ Saturn in 1997. It arrived in 2004. Through Cassini, scientists _____ seven new moons orbiting Saturn, and that one of the moons, Enceladus, may be able to support life.

3 With climate change as a growing problem, _____ is becoming more and more important. Many companies are researching and developing ways to use alternative _____, like solar and wind. Tesla Motors, a company famous for _____ very modern (but very expensive) _____ cars, is _____ another company, Panasonic, to _____ a new kind of solar tile that people can _____ on the roof of their house and get their electricity from the sun.

PRONUNCIATION

7 Listen. Underline the passive verb phrases. Then practice saying the sentences. 🎧 104

1 Electronic money is stored in Kenyans' cell phones.
2 Birds were used by the Roman army to send messages.
3 The technology was developed by scientists in Germany.
4 The first phone call was made by Alexander Graham Bell.
5 AI, or artificial intelligence, is found in most smartphones.
6 Sometimes new technologies are invented by accident.
7 The car was driven by an intelligent computer.
8 The iPhone was launched by Apple in 2007.

LISTENING

8 Listen to people talking. Which technology are they describing? Choose your answers from the options (a–f). 🎧 105

a smartphone	**d** wireless printer
b robotic worker	**e** artificial intelligence
c driverless car	**f** electronic money

1 _____   4 _____
2 _____   5 _____
3 _____   6 _____

a USB port

9 Listen. Match the products to the descriptions. 🎧 106

1 ilet 4 _____
2 Optimum 3.0 _____
3 Vertex _____
4 Optimum 5.0 _____
5 Plintar _____

a has a 17.3 inch screen
b the woman owns this laptop
c the smallest laptop
d has the longest lasting battery
e has two USB ports

landline

10 Listen to the conversation. Circle the sentence that describes how the girl's grandmother feels about new technologies. 🎧 107

1 She thinks they're too confusing.
2 She thinks they're dangerous.
3 She's not interested in them.
4 She's interested, but too busy.

11 Listen to the conversation again and answer the questions. 🎧 108

1 What does the girl find inspiring about her grandmother?
   a her kindness and generosity
   b her active lifestyle
   c her technical abilities
   d her independence

2 What problem does the girl have?
   a understanding her grandmother's life
   b getting her grandmother to respond to email
   c convincing her grandmother to get a phone
   d communicating with her grandmother

3 Why is it difficult for the girl to stay in touch with her grandmother?
   a her grandmother isn't crazy about Facebook
   b her grandmother only has a landline phone
   c her grandmother rarely turns on her computer
   d her grandmother never checks her voicemail

4 What does the granddaughter imply when she says this: "She was given a laptop for her birthday, but she has never learned to use it. I don't think she's ever even turned it on."
   a The grandmother asked for the laptop, but then changed her mind.
   b The grandmother doesn't have the time to learn how to use it.
   c The grandmother has no interest in adopting modern technology.
   d The grandmother tried to learn how to use it, but it was too difficult.

5 What does the boy suggest the girl might do?
   a teach her grandmother some tech skills
   b try to understand her grandmother's thinking
   c ask her grandmother for the new laptop
   d explain why young people do what they do

6 What does the grandmother see happening in the world?
   a people becoming less and less interested in learning
   b technology having both positive and negative effects
   c visiting people becoming more and more difficult
   d people more focused on their phones than each other

GRAMMAR The passive voice

12 Complete the sentences with the correct verb form.

1 Almost all of the 18 million smartphone users in Spain report that they *using / are used / use* apps every day.
2 A "Great Canadian Apps" section was created in the iTunes app store because so many apps *are developed / is developed / develop* in Canada.
3 A 1% tax on smartphone users in France could fund organizations that *are created / create / creating* digital content in French.
4 Nearly 25% of smartphone users in the UK said they *being / been / are* addicted to their phones.
5 In India it *reports / reported / was reported* that men use their smartphones mostly for apps and browsing the web, and women use their smartphones mostly for social media and messaging.
6 In China, more than 25% of the 246 million smartphone users regularly *using / use / is used* more than 21 apps on their phones.

13 Complete the sentence with the correct passive voice form of the verbs.

1 In 2015, more than 650,000 books _____ (publish, simple past) in the United States.
2 In the last year, print books _____ (read, simple past) by 75% of people aged 16–29.
3 E-books _____ (purchase, simple past) by 5% of adults who purchased a book last year.
4 Print books _____ (read, simple present) by 90% of people.
5 E-books _____ (buy, simple present) by fewer than 10% of readers.
6 Almost 205,000 e-books _____ (buy, simple past) in 2015, nearly 30,000 fewer than in 2014.
7 Books that _____ (price, simple present) from $3.00 to $3.99 sell better than books at any other price.
8 Sales of e-books are dropping, perhaps because more than 50,000 e-books _____ (create, simple present) each month.

14 Complete the sentences with the correct passive voice form of the verbs. Some items have more than one correct answer.

cause	earn	link	receive	(not) respond (to)
send	spend	use	write	

1 **A:** When _____ the first text message _____?
   B: The first text message _____ in 1992. It happened in the UK.
2 **A:** How much money _____ by cell phone companies from text messages each year?
   B: Cell phone companies earn $60–$70 billion each year from text messages.
3 **A:** When _____ most text messages _____?
   B: Most text messages _____ between 10:30 and 11:00pm.
4 **A:** How many text messages _____?
   B: Only 2% of text messages _____ to. That means 98% of text messages *are* responded to! Did you know that only 20% of emails are answered?
5 **A:** How many car accidents _____ to texting every year?
   B: More than 200,000 car accidents _____ by texting.

15 Change the sentences from active to passive, or from passive to active.

1 Print books are preferred by 62% of 16- to 24-year-olds in the UK.
   _____
2 In the past, books were chained to the shelves in libraries in order to stop them from being stolen.
   _____
3 The most expensive book ever purchased, Leonardo Da Vinci's *Codex Leicester*, was bought by Bill Gates for $30.8 million.
   _____
4 92% of US college students prefer print books over digital books.
   _____
5 Per capita, people in Iceland read more books than in any other country.
   _____
6 Nearly half of all magazines are bought on Friday, Saturday, and Sunday.
   _____
7 In 1949, a Spanish teacher patented the first electronic book because she wanted to reduce the number of books her students had to carry.
   _____
   _____

10B Flight of the RoboBees

VOCABULARY BUILDING

1 Complete the sentences using a form of the words in parentheses. Make changes to spelling if necessary.

1 Bees, and the work they do, helped to inspire the
_____ (develop) of small flying robots
called "RoboBees."

2 Robert Wood is a professor of _____
(engineer), as well as a National Geographic Explorer.

3 Some scientists believe that RoboBees will help with the
_____ (produce) of crops in the future.

4 The development of RoboBees is an important
_____ (achieve).

5 The _____ (develop) of the RoboBees
are a team of scientists and engineers.

READING

2 Read the article about RoboBees. Circle the TWO details
that are not mentioned by the author.

1 RoboBees have very thin wings that flap 120 times per
second.

2 Portable sources of power for RoboBees must still be
developed.

3 RoboBees might be used to pollinate a field of crops.

4 RoboBees still have to learn to communicate with each
other while working.

5 RoboBees can take off and hang in the air.

3 The article has four paragraphs (1–4). Which paragraph
contains the following information? Write the correct
number (1–4) next to each statement. You may use any
number more than once.

a how RoboBees are similar to real bees _____

b possible future use for RoboBees _____

c RoboBees are only part of the answer. _____

d Bee populations are dropping. _____

e the work of a National Geographic Explorer _____

4 Complete the summary using the passive form of the
verbs in parentheses.

RoboBees (1) _____ (develop) at the
Microrobotics Lab at Harvard University by Dr. Robert
Wood and his team. The RoboBees (2) _____
(designed) like real bees. Tasks can (3) _____
(be perform) by these robotic insects. For example, crops
could (4) _____ (pollinate) by these tiny
robots if there were not enough real bees to do the work.

5 Read the part of the article comparing RoboBees and
honeybees. Choose the correct words to complete the
sentences.

1 Wingspan is the length from the tip of one *wing /
antennae* to the tip of the other.

2 The *RoboBee / honeybee* has a larger wingspan.

3 The honeybee's wings beat more than 200 times *per
second / per minute*.

4 The *RoboBee / honeybee* is heavier.

Flight of the RoboBees

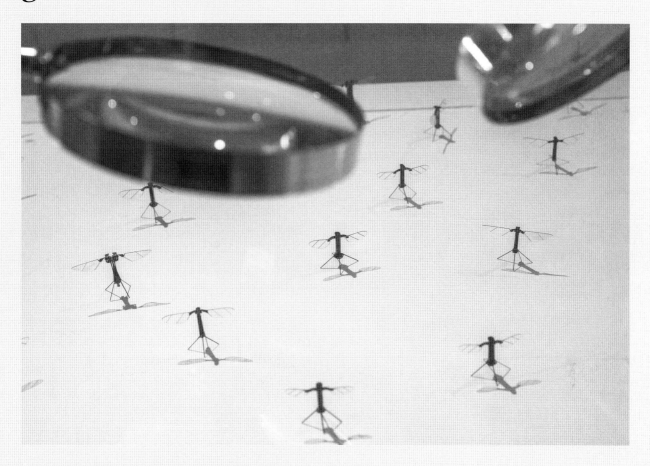

1 It's a bee! It's a robot! It's a RoboBee! A *what?* A RoboBee is a flying robot that's roughly the size of a bee or small flying insect. Like real bees, RoboBees can rise from a surface and hang in midair. They can be programmed to do tasks. They're small enough to go places real bees go and do the work of real bees.

2 The RoboBee was developed by electrical engineering professor and roboticist Robert Wood and his team at the Microrobotics Lab at Harvard University. Wood, who is also a National Geographic Explorer, is concerned about the fact that bee colonies all over the world are disappearing and bee populations are dropping dangerously. Why does that matter? Even if you don't eat honey, honeybee pollination* is incredibly important for so much of the food we eat.

3 Although RoboBees weren't developed to replace bees, roboticists like Wood believe that in the future these tiny robots might be used to pollinate a field of crops if there were a bee shortage. With two very thin wings that move rapidly—120 times per second—RoboBees can take off, and then hover in place, set down briefly, and then lift off again move to another place, as real bees do.

4 Robotic bees won't replace real bees, and we shouldn't expect them to. We still need to focus on efforts to save those vitally important creatures. But tremendous progress in the field of robotics is being made, and RoboBees are one example of how technology can help us solve problems.

RoboBees and real bees compared

RoboBee	Honeybee
Wings beat 120 times per second	Wings beat more than 200 times per second
Wingspan 3 cm	Wingspan 2.64 cm
Weight 80 mg	Weight (average) 120 mg

pollination *the process of spreading pollen in a flower*

10C Using tech to take control

GRAMMAR Passives with *by*

1 Choose the correct words to complete the sentences.

by	created	created by	invented	was	were

1 The first color TV to be patented in Mexico and the United States was invented _____ a Mexican engineer named Guillermo Gonzalez Camarena.

2 Some of the first photographs _____ developed by French-Brazilian inventor Hercules Florence.

3 The first artificial heart successfully used by a human was _____ in 1969 by Dr. Domingo Liotta, who was born in Argentina.

4 The ballpoint pen was _____ Hungarian and Argentinian journalist Laszlo Biro in the 1930s.

5 A method of changing plastic into biofuel _____ developed by Egyptian Azza Abdel Hamid Faiad.

6 A system that uses the sun's power to make water safe for drinking was _____ by Deepika Kurup.

2 Choose the correct words to complete the sentences.

1 Telescopes allow scientists to see things that can't *be seen / saw* by the human eye, such as far-off planets and stars.

2 Deserts *are thought / are thinking* by many people to be the best place to set up telescopes to look into the night sky.

3 In 1994, five men in Chile's Atacama Desert *were found / found* the highest, driest, flattest place on Earth.

4 This location in the Atacama Desert became the home of the ALMA telescope, which *is used / is using* by scientists who want answers to many questions such as how planets are born.

5 Countries in Asia, Europe, and North America *were spent / spent* $1.3 billion to establish ALMA.

6 ALMA *was planned and built / planned and built* by thousands of engineers and scientists.

3 Complete the sentences in the simple past passive voice.

1 The report _____ (write) by the student.

2 The elevator _____ (use) by people with disabilities.

3 The high mountain _____ (climb).

4 The designer's new necklace _____ (wear) by many people.

5 The bread _____ (make) by the new chefs.

6 The soup _____ (prepare) by Amy and Jai.

7 The animals at the zoo _____ (feed) by volunteers.

4 Read the questions. Complete the answers using the passive with *by*.

1 **A:** Did a lot of people see the movie?
   B: Yes! The movie _____ millions of people!

2 **A:** Did you hear that Gonzalo lost his tablet?
   B: Yes, but then it _____ (found) his teacher.

3 **A:** How many text messages did you get?
   B: Ten. But nine _____ (sent) my mother!

4 **A:** Who owns that restaurant?
   B: It _____ Mr. Ruiz.

5 **A:** How can I pay my phone bill?
   B: It can _____ check or by credit card.

6 **A:** How are sweaters made?
   B: They can _____ machine or by hand.

7 **A:** Who called the police?
   B: They _____ a man who saw the accident.

5 Read the sentences. Cross out the agent when it isn't necessary.

1 A great deal of the development of robots is done by the Japanese.
2 There are robots that can be controlled by a remote control.
3 Robots are programmed by people to do certain tasks.
4 Robots can take over some jobs that were done by people.
5 New uses for robots are found all the time by scientists.
6 The world's most expensive robot was sold last year by the company that made it.
7 Would you eat a meal that was prepared by a robot?

6 Use the prompts to write sentences in the present or past passive voice.

1 president / elect / the people (simple present passive)

2 some / of the money / spend / the actor (simple past passive)

3 lost key / find / my brother (simple past passive)

4 problem / solve / a team of students (simple past passive)

5 emergency services / contact / a woman (simple past passive)

6 children / give / shirts to wear at the competition (simple present passive)

7 project / give / to the best candidate (simple present passive)

8 messages / send / students when school is canceled (simple present passive)

7 Change the sentences from active to passive. Include the agent when necessary.

Example: People use cell phones to do more than make phone calls and send text messages.

Cell phones are used to do more than make phone calls and send text messages.

1 Because of work engineers have done, in 2015 more than 91% of the world had better sources of water to drink.

2 Energy companies are using the power of the sun to bring electricity to people in sub-Saharan Africa.

3 Eden Full, a student at Princeton University, developed solar panels that turn to face the sun for as long as possible each day.

4 Text to Change is an innovative project young people in Africa use to share their thoughts about politics and advice for the future.

10D How to control someone else's arm with your brain

TEDTALKS

AUTHENTIC LISTENING SKILLS

1 Listen to the extracts. Circle the words that have reduced forms. 🎧 110

1 All right, Sam, I'm going to record from your brain.
2 So I'm going to stand over here, and I'm going to open up our app here.
3 Do you guys want to see some more?
4 Miguel, all right. You're going to stand right here.
5 So I'm going to find your ulnar nerve, which is probably right around here.

WATCH ▶

2 Are the sentences true (T) or false (F)?

1 Neuroscientists have to go to graduate school for six and a half years. _____
2 One out of five people will have a neurological disorder—a problem with their brains. _____
3 Greg Gage made an expensive piece of equipment for studying brains in special labs. _____
4 Greg asks an audience member to try his equipment to study her own brain. _____
5 A person has about 80 billion neurons inside his brain. _____
6 Sam has heard what her brain sounds like before. _____

3 Choose the correct words to complete the sentences.

1 When Greg was a *high school* / *graduate* student, he decided to make equipment for studying the brain.
2 Greg's company is called *Backyard Brains* / *DIY Equipment*.
3 Greg's partner is named *Sam* / *Tim*.
4 Greg asks Sam to *squeeze* / *raise* her hand.
5 Greg's equipment *can* / *cannot* be carried around.

4 Choose the correct answers.

1 What is the speaker mainly discussing?
   a how universities study brains
   b how his equipment works to study the brain
   c how people develop brain problems

2 The speaker says that he made *DIY* neuroscience equipment. What is *DIY*?
   a when people make their own things
   b when people make a copy of an existing design
   c when people fix broken equipment

3 Why does the speaker mention Tim Marzullo?
   a because Tim came up with the idea by himself
   b because Tim is a graduate student
   c because Tim is his partner

4 What can be inferred about the speaker?
   a The speaker's job is to do surgeries on brains.
   b The speaker went to graduate school for six and a half years.
   c The speaker didn't graduate from college.

5 Why does the speaker say this: "This is what's happening all across the world—electrophysiology! We're going to bring on the neuro-revolution."?
   a to explain that everyone in the world is going to use only his equipment
   b to explain that there is going to be a war about neuroscience
   c to show that there is going to be a change in neuroscience

VOCABULARY IN CONTEXT

5 Choose the correct meaning of the words in bold.

1 "And one of the reasons why is that the equipment is so **complex** and so expensive that it's really only done at major universities and large institutions."
   a not simple   **b** heavy   **c** much money

2 "I need one more **volunteer**. What is your name, sir?"
   a expert
   b chance to show something
   c a person who wants to do something

3 Greg wants to show how his equipment works. He asks for Sam to **try it out**.
   a remove it
   b attempt to use it
   c get rid of it

4 "Okay, so Sam, I want you to **squeeze** your hand again."
   a raise
   b press together strongly
   c open gently

5 Greg tells Sam that after she squeezes her hand it will feel **weird** at first.
   a strange   **b** normal   **c** painful

10E Who's in control?

SPEAKING

1 Complete the sentences about studying online with the correct phrases. Then decide if each sentence is talking about pros (P), cons (C), or both sides of an argument (B).

but on the other hand
on the one hand
one bad thing about studying online
one good thing about studying online
studying online can be a problem
studying online is good

(1) _____
is that you don't have to go to school to study; you can do it whenever you want or whenever you have time. _____

(2) _____
is that it's harder to get the help you need when you have a question. Sometimes you can't ask anyone, and you always have to wait for a reply. _____

(3) _____
because you can take high-quality courses that cost less money, and some are even free! _____

(4) _____
you can study with people all over the world,

(5) _____
you don't really have anyone to work with like you do in a classroom. _____

(6) _____
because the teacher can't personalize the course for your interests, so you can lose interest and give up. _____

2 Match the sentences and responses.

1 I can't wait until we all use self-driving cars! _____

2 I don't think we need to go on vacation this year. We can just use virtual reality headsets and walk around the places in our own homes. _____

3 My brother's so popular! He's got over 3,000 friends on his social media page. _____

4 What do you think about artificial intelligence (AI) replacing humans in hospitals? _____

a OK, that's partly true, but being there yourself is good because it's the only way to experience the real life of a place.

b Really? How many of those friends does he see regularly?

c Well, on the one hand, AI can do things much more precisely, but on the other hand AI can't understand people's needs like doctors and nurses can.

d Yes, one good thing about them is that there'll be fewer accidents.

3 Over the last decade, smartphones have become an essential part of life. As with any new technology, it brings some changes that are good, and some that are bad. Make notes about the pros and cons of smartphones. Use the language you learned for talking about pros and cons. Then listen to an example of two students discussing the question, and compare this with your ideas. 🎧 **111**

Pros	Cons

4 Technology means that we use machines to make things that in the past we made by hand. Is it better to use machines to make things, or for us to do it ourselves? Make notes on your ideas and use the language you learned for talking about pros and cons. Then listen to an example of two students discussing the question. 🎧 **112**

WRITING Making a suggestion

1 Unscramble the words to make suggestions and support an argument.

1 some people / that / think most / While I understand / are noisy, I / people are not

_____

_____

2 I think / that it's / I can see / a solution / annoying, / but / we can find

_____

_____

3 try / rules / suggest / set / Can / that / of / I / a / we / different

_____

_____?

4 to / this / way / might / do / be / another / possible / It

_____

_____

2 Read the formal letter from a student, Ewa Nowak, to Mr. Herrera, the school principal. Then underline the information in 1–6 in the letter.

1 the reason for the letter
2 what the principal wants
3 the part of the rule the student agrees with
4 the name of the new set of rules suggested
5 the suggested rule about social media
6 what the new rules would allow students to do

Dear Mr. Herrera,

I'm writing about the new "no laptops" rule in the library. While I understand that you want students to read the books that are in our school library, I think laptops are extremely important study tools as well. I can see that it's a problem when some students only check social media, but most of us are studying.

Can I suggest that you replace the "no laptops" rule with a set of "serious study" rules? For example:
- The library is a place for study.
- Use laptops for research and study only.
- Respect others who are trying to study.
- Turn your laptop volume to mute.
- No checking social media in the library!

These rules would help to keep the library as a place for serious study, but would still allow students to use their laptops to research and write papers.

Thank you for considering this suggestion.

Yours sincerely,
Ewa Nowak

3 Write the missing word or words to complete the letter from Fred Evans, a student who has a part-time job at the Cozy Cafe, to Ms. Morris, the cafe owner.

but I think	can see	considering
I don't think	suggest	while
would allow	would stop	writing

Dear Ms. Morris,

I'm (1) _____ about the new "no personal phone calls" rule for employees at the Cozy Cafe. My friends and I really enjoy working at the cafe on Saturdays, but we're worried about the new rule. I (2) _____ that it gives customers a bad impression, (3) _____ we can find a solution. (4) _____ I understand that employees who spend lots of time on their cell phones at work are not doing their job properly, (5) _____ it's reasonable to ban **all** personal phone calls.

Can I (6) _____ that you replace the "no personal phone calls" rule with a new policy? For example:
- No more than two personal calls while at work.
- Speak quietly when taking any personal calls.
- Limit personal calls to five minutes, maximum.
- Do not take personal calls in front of customers.
- Additional personal calls for emergencies only!

These rules (7) _____ the annoying behavior of some employees but (8) _____ the rest of us to manage short, personal phone calls without bothering anyone.

Thank you for (9) _____ this suggestion.

Yours sincerely,
Fred Evans

4 Write a formal letter of suggestion about the following topic. Give reasons for your answer and support your idea with suggestions.

Games on cell phones are a waste of time.

From now on, there is a new rule. Students are not allowed to play games on their phones during school hours.

—Mr. Figura, School Principal

Review

1 Unscramble the words and complete the sentences.

ercasher	sveedmenoplt	rogserps
cepsors	nivnenoti	qepeminut

1 To work in a factory, you need to know how to use the

_____.

2 New _____ in face-recognition technology could make it possible for us to use our face as an ID and credit card instead of carrying a wallet around.

3 Self-driving car and truck technology is making fast _____. Soon they will be driving all around us on the roads.

4 The wheel may be the most important _____ in human history.

5 Biologists do a lot of important _____ in the rainforests to discover new species of plants and animals.

6 Introducing a new medicine to the market is a long _____ that involves years of research, development, testing, and waiting for government approval.

2 Match the sentences.

1 I created a new game to play on a cell phone. _____

2 Last year, I didn't know anything about computers. Now I can write some simple programs. _____

3 The recipe was difficult to make, but I read the instructions and did it step by step. _____

4 I have a new flying drone. I use this small device to make it go up, come down, and turn left and right. _____

5 I watched a YouTube video about building a tree house. Now I want to try it! _____

6 I want to know more about the Cassini spacecraft. _____

a I followed the process.
b I can control it.
c I've made some progress.
d I'm going to do some research.
e It's my invention.
f I need some tools and equipment.

3 Correct the passive voice errors in the sentences.

1 The number of people who own tablet computers predicted to reach 150 million very soon.

_____

2 Nearly 14 hours a week on average is spent using tablets, more than smartphones and PCs. _____

3 Tablets was use by most people on weekdays, not weekends. _____

4 Nearly half of tablets are share by more than one person, but only one third of people share their smartphones.

_____

5 Wifi-only tablets is preferred by most people, rather than 4G tablets. _____

6 It expects that PC usage will decrease in the next five years as tablet use increases. _____

4 Choose the correct words to complete the sentences.

1 The Bay of Bengal *was seen / saw* by the tourists.
2 The coach *was given / gave* the instructions.
3 Rena *was spent / spent* the money.
4 We *are seen / saw* several gas stations along the road to the airport.

5 Look at the photos. Write three or four sentences about each one using the passive.

Example: The *Titanic*

This ship was named the Titanic *because of its size. It was built in England and was launched in the Atlantic in 1912. It was sunk on its first voyage and can only be seen now under the sea!*

The Sphinx

The Great Wall

Machu Picchu

UNIT 6

Review

afraid (adj)	/əˈfreɪd/
friendly (adj)	/ˈfrɛndli/
nervous (adj)	/ˈnɜrvəs/
relaxed (adj)	/rəˈlækst/
shy (adj)	/ʃaɪ/
worried (adj)	/ˈwʌrid/

Unit Vocabulary

accept (v)	/ɪkˈsɛpt/
fail (v)	/ˈfeɪl/
failure (n)	/ˈfeɪljər/
imperfect (adj)	/ɪmˈpɜrfɪkt/
imperfection (n)	/ˌɪmpərˈfɛkʃən/
perfect (adj)	/ˈpɜrfɛkt/
perfection (n)	/pərˈfɛkʃən/
reject (v)	/rɪˈdʒɛkt/
success (n)	/səkˈsɛs/
succeed (v)	/səkˈsid/
successful (adj)	/səkˈsɛsfəl/
unsuccessful (adj)	/ˌʌnsəkˈsɛsfəl/

Extension

academic success (n)	/ækəˈdɛmɪk/ /səkˈsɛs/
accept responsibility (phrase)	/ɪkˈsɛpt/ /rɪspɑnsəˈbɪləti/
condition (n)	/kənˈdɪʃən/
economic success (phrase)	/ɛkəˈnɑmɪk/ /səkˈsɛs/
failed two exams (phrase)	/ˈfeɪld/ /tu/ /ɪgˈzæmz/
perfect example (phrase)	/ˈpɜrfɪkt/ /ɪgˈzæmpəl/
perfect opportunity (phrase)	/ˈpɜrfɪkt/ /ɑpərˈtunəti/
reject an idea (phrase) (phrase)	/rɪˈdʒɛkt/ /ən/ /aɪˈdiə/
slightly imperfect	/ˈslaɪtli/ /ɪmˈpɜrfɪkt/
successful company (phrase)	/səkˈsɛsfəl/ /ˈkʌmpəni/
very successful (phrase)	/ˈvɛri/ /səkˈsɛsfəl/

Vocabulary Building

disagree (v)	/ˌdɪsəˈgri/
disconnect (v)	/dɪskəˈnɛkt/
dishonest	/dɪsˈɑnəst/
dislike (v)	/dɪsˈlaɪk/
immature (adj)	/ɪməˈtʊr/
improper (adj)	/ɪmˈprɑpər/
inactive (adj)	/ɪnˈæktɪv/
incorrect (adj)	/ɪnkərˈrɛkt/
indirect (adj)	/ɪndərˈrɛkt/
unfinished (adj)	/ʌnˈfɪnɪʃt/
unkind (adj)	/ʌnˈkaɪnd/
unlucky (adj)	/ʌnˈlʌki/
unsuccessful (adj)	/ʌnsəkˈsɛsfəl/

Vocabulary in Context

courageous (adj)	/kəˈreɪdʒəs/
negotiate (v)	/nɪˈgoʊʃieɪt/
potential (adj)	/pəˈtɛnʃəl/
ran (v)	/ˈræn/
struggling (v)	/ˈstrʌɡəlɪŋ/
supportive network (adj)-(n) (collocation)	/səˈpɔrtɪv/ /ˈnɛtwərk/

UNIT 7

Review

bananas (n)	/bəˈnænəz/
bread (n)	/ˈbrɛd/
butter (n)	/ˈbʌtər/
breakfast (n)	/ˈbrɛkfəst/
cake (n)	/ˈkeɪk/
cheese (n)	/ˈtʃiz/
dinner (n)	/ˈdɪnər/
eggs (n)	/ˈɛgz/
fish (n)	/ˈfɪʃ/
lunch (n)	/ˈlʌntʃ/
milk (n)	/ˈmɪlk/
orange juice (n)	/ˈɑrɪndʒ/ /ˈdʒus/
pizza (n)	/ˈpitsə/
rice (n)	/ˈraɪs/
salad (n)	/ˈsæləd/
sandwich (n)	/ˈsændwɪtʃ/
sauce (n)	/ˈsɔs/
soup (n)	/ˈsup/
sugar (n)	/ˈʃʊgər/

Unit Vocabulary

apple (n)	/ˈæpəl/
bitter (adj)	/ˈbɪtər/
cafe (n)	/kæˈfeɪ/
chicken (n)	/ˈtʃɪkɪn/
chili powder (n)	/ˈtʃɪli ˌpaʊdər/
chocolate (n)	/ˈtʃɔklət/
choose (v)	/ˈtʃuz/
dessert (n)	/dɪˈzɜrt/
dish (n)	/ˈdɪʃ/
drink (n)	/drɪŋk/
eat (v)	/ˈit/
flavor (n)	/ˈfleɪvər/
french fries (n)	/ˈfrɛntʃ/ /ˈfraɪz/
fruit (n)	/ˈfrut/
fruit salad (n)	/ˈfrut/ /ˈsæləd/
hungry (adj)	/ˈhʌŋgri/
ice cream (n)	/ˈaɪs ˌkrim/
ingredient (n)	/ɪnˈgridiənt/
lemon (n)	/ˈlɛmən/
meat (n)	/ˈmit/
order (v)	/ˈɔrdər/
pasta (n)	/ˈpɑstə/
potato (n)	/pəˈteɪtoʊ/
prepare (v)	/prɪˈpɛr/

salty (adj)	/ˈsɔlti/
sandwich (n)	/ˈsændwɪtʃ/
section (n)	/ˈsɛkʃən/
shrimp (n)	/ˈʃrɪmp/
snack (n)	/ˈsnæk/
sour (adj)	/saʊr/
spice (n)	/spaɪs/
spicy (adj)	/ˈspaɪsi/
strawberry (n)	/ˈstrɔˌbɛri/
sweet (adj)	/swit/
tomato (n)	/təˈmeɪtoʊ/
vegetable (n)	/ˈvɛdʒtəbəl/

Extension

amount (n)	/əˈmaʊnt/
boiled (adj)	/ˈbɔɪld/
delicious (adj)	/dɪˈlɪʃəs/
fast food (n)	/ˈfæst/ /ˈfud/
fresh (adj)	/ˈfrɛʃ/
fried (adj)	/ˈfraɪd/
frozen food (n)	/ˈfroʊzn/ /ˈfud/
grilled (adj)	/ˈgrɪld/
home-cooked meal (n)	/ˈhoʊmˈkʊkt/ /ˈmil/
huge (adj)	/ˈhjudʒ/
natural (adj)	/ˈnætʃərəl/
taste (n)	/ˈteɪst/
terrible (adj)	/ˈtɛrəbəl/
unhealthy (adj)	/ʌnˈhɛlθi/

Vocabulary Building

accomplishment (n)	/əˈkɑmplɪʃmənt/
development (n)	/dɪˈvɛləpmənt/
disappearance (n)	/dɪsəˈpɪrəns/
farmer (n)	/ˈfɑrmər/
planners (n)	/ˈplænərz/

Vocabulary in Context

global (adj)	/ˈgloʊbəl/
households (n)	/ˈhaʊshoʊldz/
invested (v)	/ɪnˈvɛstəd/
resources (n)	/ˈrisɔrsəz/
tackle (v)	/ˈtækəl/

UNIT 8

Review

cheap (adj)	/ˈtʃip/
customer (n)	/ˈkʌstəmər/
department store (n)	/dɪˈpɑrtmənt/ /ˈstɔr/
(not) for sale (phrase)	/ˈnɑt/ /ˈfɔr/ /ˈseɪl/
expensive (adj)	/ɪkˈspɛnsɪv/
market (n)	/ˈmɑrkət/
price (n)	/ˈpraɪs/
price tag (n)	/ˈpraɪs/ /ˈtæg/
save money (phrase)	/ˈseɪv/ /ˈmʌni/

shop online (v)	/'ʃɑp/ /'ɔnlaɪn/
shoppers (n)	/'ʃɑpərz/
shopping mall (n)	/'ʃɑpɪŋ/ /'mɔl/
spend money (phrase)	/'spɛnd/ /'mʌni/

Unit Vocabulary

advertise (v)	/'ædvərtaɪz/
design (v)	/dɪ'zaɪn/
grow (v)	/'groʊ/
manufacture (v)	/ˌmænjə'fæktʃər/
material (n)	/mə'tɪriəl/
option (n)	/'ɑpʃən/
pick (v)	/pɪk/
produce (v)	/prə'dus/
recycle (v)	/ˌri'saɪkəl/
sell (v)	/sɛl/
throw away (v)	/'θroʊ/ /ə'weɪ/

Extension

afford (v)	/ə'fɔrd/
antique (adj)	/æn'tik/
bargain (n)	/'bɑrgən/
billboards (n)	/'bɪlbɔrdz/
delivered (adj)	/dɪ'lɪvərd/
discount (adj)	/'dɪskaʊnt/
display (n)	/dɪ'spleɪ/
second-hand (adj)	/'sɛkənd-'hænd/
trade (v)	/'treɪd/

Vocabulary Building

air pollution (n)	/ɛr/ /pə'luʃən/
billboards (n)	/'bɪlbɔrdz/
sea life (n)	/'si/ /'laɪf/
shopping mall (n)	/'ʃɑpɪŋ/ /'mɔl/
supermarket (n)	/'supərmɑrkət/
TV shows (n)	/'ti'vi/ /'ʃoʊz/
video games (n)	/'vɪdioʊ/ /'geɪmz/
website (n)	/'wɛbsaɪt/

Vocabulary in Context

cause a change (phrase)	/'kɔz/ /ə/ /'tʃeɪndʒ/
do as you say (phrase)	/'du/ /'æz/ /'ju/ /'seɪ/
in a way that (phrase)	/'ɪn/ /ə/ /'weɪ/ /'ðæt/
take action (phrase)	/'teɪk/ /'ækʃən/

UNIT 9

Review

actor (n)	/'æktər/
artist (n)	/'ɑrtɪst/
boss (n)	/'bɑs/
businessperson (n)	/'bɪznəspɜrsn̩/
businesswoman (n)	/'bɪznəswʊmən/
cook (n)	/'kʊk/
driver (n)	/'draɪvər/
guide (n)	/'gaɪd/
farmer (n)	/'fɑrmər/
photographer (n)	/fə'tɑgrəfər/
receptionist (n)	/rɪ'sɛpʃənɪst/
teacher (n)	/'titʃər/

| tour guide (n) | /'tʊr/ /'gaɪd/ |
| waiter / waitress (n) | /'weɪtər/ /'weɪtrəs/ |

Unit Vocabulary

accountant (n)	/ə'kaʊntənt/
architect (n)	/'ɑrkətɛkt/
chef (n)	/ʃɛf/
chief executive (n)	/tʃif/ /ɪg'zɛk.jə.t̬ɪv/
cleaner (n)	/'klinər/
construction worker (n)	/kən'strʌkʃən/ /'wɜrkər/
doctor (n)	/'dɑktər/
electronics engineer (n)	/ɪlɛk'trɑnɪks/ /ɛndʒə'nɪr/
factory worker (n)	/'fæktəri/ /'wɜrkər/
lawyer (n)	/'lɔɪər/
manager (n)	/'mænədʒər/
nurse (n)	/nɜrs/
office worker (n)	/'ɑfəs/ /'wɜrkər/
paramedic (n)	/ˌpærə'mɛdɪk/
police officer (n)	/pə'lis,ɑfɪsər/
salesperson (n)	/'seɪlz,pɜrsən/
software engineer (n)	/'sɔftwɛr/ /ˌɛndʒɪnɪr/
store manager (n)	/stɔr/ /'mænədʒər/

Extension

adventure (n)	/əd'vɛntʃər/
assistant (n)	/ə'sɪstənt/
application (n)	/æplə'keɪʃən/
benefit (n)	/'bɛnəfɪt/
career (n)	/kər'rɪr/
challenge (n)	/'tʃæləndʒ/
employed (adj)	/ɪm'plɔɪd/
employment (n)	/ɪm'plɔɪmənt/
excitement (n)	/ɪk'saɪtmənt/
an expert (n)	/ən/ /'ɛkspɜrt/
freedom (n)	/'fridəm/
full-time (adj)	/'fʊl'taɪm/
get a job (phrase)	/'gɛt/ /ə/ /'dʒɑb/
a hard worker (phrase)	/ə/ /'hɑrd/ /'wɜrkər/
in charge (adj)	/'ɪn/ /'tʃɑrdʒ/
internship (n)	/'ɪntɜrnʃɪp/
opportunity (n)	/ɑpər'tunəti/
out of work (adj)	/'aʊt/ /əv/ /'wɜrk/
professional (adj)	/prə'fɛʃənl̩/
resume (n)	/rɛ'zumeɪ/
salary (n)	/'sæləri/
unemployed (adj)	/ʌnɪm'plɔɪd/

Vocabulary Building

borrow from (v)	/'bɑroʊ/ /frəm/
take from (v)	/'teɪk/ /frəm/
use in (v)	/'juz/ /'ɪn/
work on (v)	/'wɜrk/ /'ɑn/

Vocabulary in Context

curiosity (adj)	/kjʊri'ɑsəti/
focus on (v)	/'foʊkəs/ /'ɑn/
freedom (n)	/'fridəm/

global (adj)	/'gloʊbəl/
tough (adj)	/'tʌf/
use up (v)	/'juz/ /'ʌp/

UNIT 10

Review

camera (n)	/'kæmrə/
cell phone (n)	/'sɛl/ /'foʊn/
computer (n)	/kəm'pjutər/
machine (n)	/mə'ʃin/
printer (n)	/'prɪntər/
program (n)	/'proʊgræm/
tablet (n)	/'tæblət/
texts (n)	/'tɛksts/
video game (n)	/'vɪdioʊ/ /'geɪm/

Unit Vocabulary

control (v)	/kən'troʊl/
development (n)	/dɪ'vɛləpmənt/
equipment (n)	/ɪ'kwɪpmənt/
inventions (n)	/ɪn'vɛnʃənz/
micro-robot (n)	/'maɪkro'roʊbɑt/
process (n)	/'prɑsɛs/
progress (n)	/'prɑgrɛs/
remote control (n)	/rɪ'moʊt/ /kən'troʊl/
research (n)	/'risɜrtʃ/
robot (n)	/'roʊbɑt/
technology (n)	/tɛk'nɑlədʒi/
tool (n)	/'tul/

Extension

design (v)	/dɪ'zaɪn/
discover (v)	/dɪ'skʌvər/
energy (n)	/'ɛnərdʒi/
explore (v)	/ɪk'splɔr/
green technology (n)	/'grin/ /tɛk'nɑlədʒi/
install (v)	/ɪn'stɔl/
partner (with) (v)	/'pɑrtnər/ /'wɪθ/
spacecraft (n)	/'speɪskræft/

Vocabulary Building

achievement (n)	/ə'tʃivmənt/
developer (n)	/dɪ'vɛləpər/
development (n)	/dɪ'vɛləpmənt/
engineering (n)	/ɛndʒə'nɪrɪŋ/
production (n)	/prə'dʌkʃən/

Vocabulary in Context

complex (adj)	/kɑm'plɛks/
squeeze (v)	/skwiz/
try it out (v)	/traɪ/ /ɪt/ /aʊt/
volunteer (n)	/ˌvɑlən'tɪr/
weird (adj)	/wɪrd/

PHOTO CREDITS